What Are Global Warming and Climate Change?

What Are Global Warming and Climate Change?

Answers For Young Readers

CHUCK MCCUTCHEON

University of New Mexico Press   Albuquerque

Barbara Guth Worlds of Wonder

Science Series for Young Readers

Advisory Editors: David Holtby and Karen Taschek

Please see page 104 for more information about the series.

Printed in China by Four Colour Print Group
Production location: Guangdong, China | Date of Production: 1/27/2010 | Cohort: Batch I

15 14 13 12 11 10   1 2 3 4 5 6

LIBRARY OF CONGRESS CATALOGING-IN-PUBLICATION DATA

McCutcheon, Chuck, 1963–
What are global warming and climate change? : answers for young readers /
Chuck McCutcheon.
p. cm. — (Barbara Guth worlds of wonder science series for young readers)
Includes index.
ISBN 978-0-8263-4745-9 (cloth : alk. paper)
1. Global warming—Juvenile literature. 2. Greenhouse effect, Atmospheric—
Juvenile literature. 3. Climatic changes—Juvenile literature. I. Title.
QC981.8.G56M39 2010
363.738'74—dc22
                                        2009035826

In memory of Dave Holden and Fran McCutcheon

Contents

Acknowledgments

Some brief thanks: to David Holtby, for approaching me about writing a book for this important series; to the many scientists, students, environmentalists, congressional staffers, journalists, bloggers, and others who took time to provide thoughts on how best to communicate this subject to this audience; to Judi Hasson, for her usual sharp editing advice; and to my wife, Liisa, for putting up with me during this whole process.

Introduction

What's This Book About?

You've probably heard *something's* happening.

Maybe you've learned about massive glaciers melting or looked at photos of animals and birds atop chunks of melting ice. You also might have seen news stories about extreme events—hurricanes, floods, water shortages, heat waves, electricity blackouts—and heard experts wonder about whether more are coming. You may have

A seal atop a patch of melting ice.

listened to politicians throwing around words like *emergency, disaster,* and *catastrophe.*

Global warming is real. It has become a big deal, and it's going to remain that way for many years. The earth's surface temperature, which hasn't changed much in 10,000 years, has shot up during the last few decades. Nearly every part of the planet has gotten warmer.

"The earth has a fever, and the fever is rising," says former vice president Al Gore, who won a Nobel Prize for his work on this issue.

If the fever continues, we won't be able to adapt fast enough. Many types of plants and animals will have trouble too. Our lives will change—not just in places where it's cold now, but almost everywhere.

You might think global warming is going to be like some scary movie where everything happens in an instant. It won't. Coastal cities won't suddenly be underwater, and we won't be burned to a crisp the second we step outdoors. Weather-related problems will occur gradually—more heat waves with temperatures over 100 degrees Fahrenheit (F.) (38 degrees Celsius, C.), more drought, rising sea levels, and other problems.

"We are all used to talking about these impacts coming in the lifetimes of our children and grandchildren," said Martin Parry, who cochaired the Intergovernmental Panel on Climate Change, the main scientific group studying this problem. "Now we know that it's us."

But we can do something about it.

Many things can help. They range from simple steps, like changing kinds of lightbulbs and lowering the thermostat, to more complex options, like negotiating agreements with other countries to limit *emissions* of the gases that are the cause of global warming. New technologies to fight the problem are being developed. All of these things have their limits; no one of them, by itself, will solve a problem that is so severe it wouldn't end even if we somehow were able to magically halt all emissions tomorrow. But people still need to take global warming seriously.

If you'd like to be one of those people—or just want to learn more about this topic—then this book is for you. It's intended as an easy-to-understand guide to what is possibly the most important subject of our time. Activities at the end of some chapters will help increase your knowledge about global warming.

What is global warming?

Global warming describes what makes the world a hotter place—the increase in temperature of the earth's air and oceans.

The earth has a natural process of setting its thermostat. Atmospheric gases—commonly called greenhouse gases—warm the *atmosphere* and surface. This *greenhouse effect* allows us to live on the earth. But the balance of gases in the atmosphere, the extremely thin layer of air surrounding the earth, is being disrupted by human activity. That has led to warmer temperatures, leading to a change in climate.

The situation is often compared to a blanket around the earth. The blanket is made up of gases that have been collecting in the atmosphere. The sun's heat gets trapped underneath that blanket—but the blanket is getting thicker, making it hard for the earth to cool down. So temperatures get warmer and warmer.

How is global warming different from climate change?

Global warming refers to the increase in the average temperature of the earth over several years or decades. *Climate change* refers to both global warming and other changes in climate that accompany the warming. These changes include more common and more intense extreme weather and a rise in sea levels.

Many people see global warming and climate change as the same. But some experts consider the word *warming* misleading because it doesn't include the full range of changes. Also, they think it doesn't make people care enough about the problem. As National Aeronautics and Space Administration (NASA) climate scientist Drew Shindell told the newspaper the *New York Times*: "Global warming sounds cozy and comfortable."

Some scientists prefer the terms *global heating* or *global climate disruption.* A few even suggest *global weirding* because of the weird things that are going to happen.

Is climate change caused by things other than people?

Yes. But people have been speeding up the warming by burning fossil fuels—coal, oil, and natural gas—and cutting down forests. Scientists have found that these activities are pumping far more carbon dioxide (the main source of the problem) and other greenhouse gases into the atmosphere. Within the last couple of decades, records have repeatedly been set for the warmest years on record—and then broken the next year or the year after that.

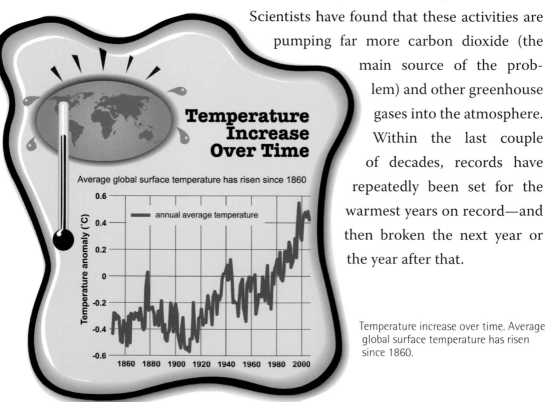

Temperature Increase Over Time

Average global surface temperature has risen since 1860

Temperature anomaly (°C)

— annual average temperature

Temperature increase over time. Average global surface temperature has risen since 1860.

Are people definitely responsible for what's happening?

An overwhelming majority of scientists say yes.

The Intergovernmental Panel on Climate Change is made up of hundreds of scientists from the United States and other countries. In its 2007 report, the panel said that warming of the climate system is "unequivocal" (definite) and went on to say that it had "very high confidence" human activities had contributed to global warming. Translated, that means there's at least a nine out of 10 chance that human activity is the correct explanation for global warming.

And that panel isn't alone in its conclusions. The U.S. Global Change Research Program, an team of government scientists, said in a 2009 report: "The global warming observed over the past 50 years is due primarily to human-induced emissions of heat-trapping gases."

The American Geophysical Union, an international scientific society with more than 35,000 members, said, "Natural influences cannot explain the rapid increase in global near-surface temperatures." And the science academies of the United States and 10 other countries put out a statement in 2005 that said: "It is likely that most of the warming in recent decades can be attributed to human activities." Since then, it has published more statements backing that up.

Naomi Oreskes, a professor at the University of California at San Diego, studied more than 900 articles on climate change published in serious scientific journals between 1993 and 2003. Three-quarters of the articles endorsed the idea that humans were responsible for at least some of the global warming of the past 50 years. The others took no position. Not a single one challenged the idea that human-caused global warming is occurring. All of this has led many to accept that people are responsible for global warming.

How much is the temperature going up?

Since 1900, the average global temperature already has gone up about 1.5 degrees F. (0.8 degrees C.). Although it's hard to predict future greenhouse gas levels, the earth will probably warm somewhere between another two and 11.5 degrees F. (1.1 and 6.4 degrees C.) by 2100. Even if we stopped emitting heat-trapping gases immediately, the climate would still continue to warm for many decades because the gases already released into the atmosphere will stay there for years— even centuries. This means we should act sooner rather than later.

Would a temperature rise of just a couple of degrees really have that big an effect?

Yes. It won't just make things more pleasantly warm. Over the last 10,000 years, the earth's average temperature hasn't varied by more than 1.8 degrees F. (1 degree C.). People, plants, and animals have gotten used to those relatively stable conditions.

Temperatures now are only five to nine degrees F. (three to five degrees C.) warmer than the days at the end of the last *ice age*, in which much of the northern United States, Europe, and Asia was covered by more than 3,000 feet (914 meters) of ice. So a small temperature change will throw the climate out of balance.

Will all this mean I can get a suntan in the middle of winter?

Not really. The sun isn't a major contributor to global warming. But if it warms up enough in winter to where it's like summer, you might.

Why do some people say global warming isn't happening?

Science doesn't often produce a single universally agreed-on answer. Sometimes its results can be interpreted in different ways. A few scientists look at those results differently from the vast majority of other scientists.

Natural cycles of warming and cooling have taken place throughout history. Some people say this means there's no evidence that recent global warming is part of a natural cycle. But most of the scientific world disagrees with them.

Many people who deny that global warming is taking place don't submit their findings to other scientists to review before they publish those findings. Some of these people aren't entirely honest—they may have been paid by the oil, mining, and other industries that have a vested interest in denying climate change.

Global warming has greatly affected polar bears.

Other people say that global warming is occurring but the role of human activity isn't clear or fully proven. They say nature might play a bigger role in causing higher temperatures than humanity does. For example, they say the amount of energy given off by the sun may be increasing. But recent measurements show that the sun's energy has added only slightly to recent warming during the first half of the last century and not at all to the rapid warming of recent years.

Even people who do accept that humans have contributed to climate change sometimes say that scientists, the media, and others have overreacted. They argue that global warming isn't the huge problem it's portrayed to be. These people worry more about how much taking action to prevent climate change will cost—for example, in paying extra taxes—as much or more than its environmental impacts. So they oppose taking steps to reduce warming, such as signing international treaties, that they say could do more harm than good, especially to the economy.

What do most Americans think?

Increased news reporting about global warming, along with books, TV shows, and movies, like Al Gore's movie *An Inconvenient Truth*, have caused Americans to recognize the problem of global warming.

In 1992, according to one poll, about one out of every four people admitted they didn't know anything about global warming. Fifteen years later, in 2007, that figure was down to about one out of every 25 people.

Also in 2007, one-third of Americans told pollsters that global warming is the world's biggest environmental problem. That was twice the number who gave it the top ranking a year earlier. Since then, though, other polls have shown that people haven't made it a huge priority. A 2009 Gallup Poll found global warming came in last

The 2007 Live Earth concert in London entertained people while informing them about global warming.

compared to eight other environmental concerns that people said they worried about a great deal or a fair amount, including water pollution, air pollution, and the extinction of plants and animals.

What about younger people?

Schools are teaching more about climate change, and celebrities like actor Leonardo DiCaprio are taking up the cause. Increasing numbers of young adults see climate change as their generation's biggest problem. In 2007, the Live Earth series of concerts around the world attracted dozens of performers, including Madonna, Snoop Dogg, Kanye West, and Alicia Keys, to draw attention to the issue. Polls show adults between ages 18 and 29 are more attuned to the threat than older adults.

Even so, many young people still think climate change is far off. A national survey of 900 high school students in 2007 found that only about a quarter of them believe climate change is very likely to affect them personally in their lifetimes.

What do scientific experts think should be done?

The experts say we should produce less carbon dioxide and other greenhouse gases by burning less coal, gas, and oil—and that we should do it in a very short time. The Intergovernmental Panel on Climate Change said in 2007 that the world will have to become mostly free of carbon-emitting technologies in about four decades to avoid widespread extinctions of animal species, decreased food production, flooding for millions of people, and higher deaths from heat waves. To do that, people all over the world need to change their lifestyles, and governments need to take the problem seriously.

We'll cover the thinking behind how we reached this point and what else is being done to address the problem of climate change in the chapters ahead.

CHAPTER 1

What Is Climate, Anyway?

Is climate the same as weather?

Not exactly. *Weather* is whatever is happening outdoors. It's what occurs from minute to minute—daily changes in rain and snow, temperature and wind conditions. We experience weather locally, at one place and at one time.

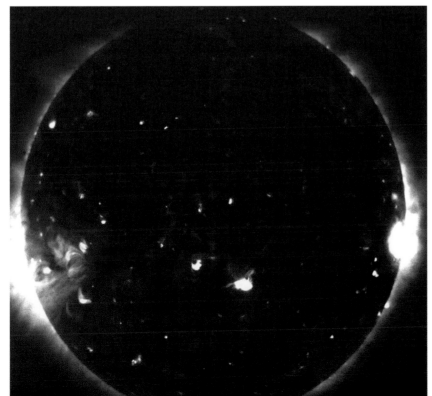

The sun.

The sun reflecting off ice.

Climate describes weather occurring over longer periods—usually at least a few weeks—in a given place. This includes average weather conditions, regular weather sequences (like the seasons), and special weather events (like tornadoes and floods).

You can make generalizations about a city or a region's weather based on its climate: Buffalo has a snowy climate. Seattle has a rainy one. Florida has a warm one.

Because weather is so chaotic, it's often hard to predict beyond a few days—or sometimes even a few hours in advance. But projecting longer-term changes in climate is a more manageable issue. Think of it this way: it's almost impossible to foresee the age at which an individual person might die. But looking at a broader set of information, we can say with confidence that the average age of death for men in countries like the United States is around 75.

What determines climate?

It's created by complex relationships between the components that make up the climate system—the sun, the atmosphere, water, land, ocean, ice, and biosphere (the areas on the earth where living things are found). Places near the ocean, for example, tend to have more moderate climates than those far from the coasts.

What's the role of the sun?

Nearly all of the earth's energy comes from the sun, even if some of it is indirect. When sunlight hits the earth, some of it gets reflected back into space. But the rest gets absorbed by the earth's surface and turned into heat. This heat is what ultimately drives the wind patterns, ocean currents, and other aspects of the earth's climate.

What about the other areas of the climate system?

The atmosphere is the very thin blanket of air surrounding the earth. It's made up mostly of nitrogen and oxygen. A variety of other gases make up the remaining 1 percent. Those gases create a natural phenomenon known as the *greenhouse effect*, which is central to understanding global warming. We'll talk more about it in the next chapter.

The land areas of the earth also affect climate. Temperatures are more extreme in the middle of large masses of land. Mountains force the air that hits them to rise so the water *vapor* condenses into clouds, which in turn release their water as rain and snow.

Ice has a big effect on climate. Ice has a greater *albedo*—the ability to reflect light that falls on it—than land or oceans. Freshly fallen snow has the highest albedo of all, reflecting 80 percent or more of the light that hits it back into space before it can turn into heat.

Snowfall that gives the earth's surface a high albedo level is an example of what scientists call *positive feedback*. *Feedbacks* are factors that tend to affect climate.

A *feedback loop* is a pattern of interacting processes where a change in one area can cause other changes. A feedback loop works like this: as the frozen sea surface of an ocean melts to water, there is less white to reflect the sun's heat back into space—and more dark, open water to absorb that heat, which then melts the floating sea ice even faster.

What has the climate been like over time?

Our climate has been constantly changing since the earth began, with periods of global warming and global cooling long before human beings and their activities began. The orbits of the sun and earth undergo a variety of changes over time. Even tiny changes in the tilt of the earth and the shape of its orbit around the sun can make a big difference in global climate.

In fact, the earth has been warming and cooling in fairly regular cycles for about 2.5 million years. After a warm period of about 10,000 years, the earth has plunged into an ice age, then slowly recovered through a warming trend that kept getting warmer—until another ice age began.

What about before we entered this interglacial period?

The temperature shifted back and forth. Nearly 13,000 years ago, in the middle of a warming trend, it suddenly became much colder—during the event known as the Younger Dryas or the "Big Freeze," Europe was about 12 to 16 degrees F. (6.7 to 8.9 degrees C.) colder than today—and it stayed that way for 1,200 years.

The Younger Dryas is named after the dryas plant, a little rose that is now found only on treeless plains near the polar ice but that once reached all the way south into Virginia. The event led to the extinction of early animals like mammoths and saber-toothed tigers.

Scientists have spent much time trying to explain this. One theory is that the Younger Dryas was caused by a significant reduction or a shutdown of the North Atlantic thermohaline circulation—a conveyor-belt-like current in the deep sea that connects the major oceans. Others say a comet hurtled toward the earth, fractured into pieces, and exploded into fireballs, causing fires that killed animals.

We haven't had anything comparable in scale to the Younger Dryas since then. But scientists wonder if recent global warming could ever lead to another, similar event.

Researchers collect numerous ice core samples for study.

How do we know what the earth and its climate were like before thermometers were invented?

Even though global temperatures have only been systematically measured since 1861, humans have been recording evidence of climate changes for thousands of years.

In the Sahara desert, ancient rock carvings showing a fertile landscape full of giraffes and other animals are a sign that once there were enough plants and water for wildlife. Drawings of hippopotamuses, which need water year-round, have been found in other areas that now are *barren*.

Some clues come from the earth itself. Natural recorders of climate variations are called *proxies*. They include ocean and lake sediments, ice cores (tubes of ice extracted from under the surface with an ice drill showing years' worth of snow and ice information), fossils, tree rings, and corals.

Through these proxies, scientists can make educated guesses at long-term regional temperature trends as well as changes in the atmosphere's chemical makeup. For example:

* Tree rings can show what climate factors shaped each year of a tree's life.
* Bubbles trapped inside ice fields hold air from thousands of years ago that can be analyzed to determine the climate when the ice fell as snow.
* Shells and other debris deposited in layers of sediment on the bottom of lakes and oceans can be analyzed to provide insights into past climate.

How are future climate changes predicted?

In a variety of ways. Scientists study climate patterns of both the past and the present. They also study the factors that are part of the climate, including ocean surface temperatures and currents, winds, and the amount of greenhouse gases and dust that are in the atmosphere. They try to figure out what will happen to the climate if those factors change, along with what happens to them when the climate starts shifting.

Information is fed into a computer to develop a model. The models can't predict exactly what will happen, but as computers have become faster, climate modeling has made big advances. The first

Clouds.

successful weather forecast was done in 1950 on a computer that made 5,000 calculations per second. Today's fastest computers can do trillions of calculations per second.

How do the models work?

Computer models divide the atmosphere and oceans into a number of boxes, or cells. Each cell represents an area that is a couple of miles high and hundreds of miles wide. Each cell is given a certain temperature, humidity, wind speed and direction, and so on to start. The program also includes a set of equations that connects the cells by describing the way changes in one cell affect changes in others around it. Programmers then run these programs forward in time to see how the climate system changes.

The computer models examine many aspects of the climate system, including ocean surface temperatures and currents, wind direction and speed, and the amount of greenhouse gases and dust in the atmosphere. Scientists generally are more confident in estimating some variables (like the temperature) than others (like the amount of precipitation).

How do scientists know when a climate model is accurate?

One way is to have the model calculate past climates. That allows the scientists to check their results against the historical record. If the scientists' predictions match what actually happened, they have confidence in the model.

Why can't climate models predict climate change perfectly?

There are many reasons, but one is that all models have to take uncertainty into account. The biggest uncertainty is that we don't know what future greenhouse gas emissions will be.

Weather satellites capture important climate data.

Clouds are another big uncertainty in modeling climate change. Clouds affect the sun's energy coming in as well as the heat either going out or staying near the earth. But computers have a hard time simulating them.

Just because there's some uncertainty in the models, though, doesn't mean we can't trust their results. Sophisticated models developed within the last two decades represent the physical processes that are thought to be an important measurement of the actual climate and have done a good job explaining the changes that have taken place.

What's the role of satellites in determining whether global warming exists?

Satellites have helped greatly in making readings of the earth's temperature more accurate and in gathering other information. But satellites have only been used in a serious way to study climate for about the last 30 years. Scientists have said they wish they had satellite data for the last 200 years for the entire globe. That, they say, would help convince people of the longer-term patterns showing shifts in climate.

Satellites can measure temperatures in the lower atmosphere (less than six miles, or 9.7 kilometers, aboveground), while surface temperature measurements are made just a few feet (about a meter) from the surface.

Until recently, conflicting studies suggested that temperatures measured by satellites revealed a slight cooling trend, while the surface temperature record showed a warming trend. This has caused a lot of controversy. Scientists eventually found that they neglected some measurement and calibration problems with the satellites, including the fact that satellites were falling from their orbits instead of being where they were expected to be. Correcting these problems revealed a warming trend that is closer to what surface measurements have picked up.

Was it colder during the 1970s?

Skeptics of climate change sometimes cite the 1970s as evidence that climate change happens in cycles and is not caused by the burning of fossil fuels like oil and coal. The 1970s was a very cold decade compared to the ones before it, and news stories sometimes talked about the possibility of a "new ice age."

But in dozens of scientific articles written between 1965 and 1979, most scientists predicted global warming and only a few supported global cooling.

So tell me again: if we can't predict the weather 10 days in advance, how can we predict the climate 100 years from now?

Weather forecasting and climate projections are very different. Weather forecasting is based mainly on the movements and interactions of weather details like storm fronts and air patterns. Climate projections are based mainly on the physics of long-term changes in solar energy and radiation—a subject we'll go into more in the next chapter.

CHAPTER 2

What's the Greenhouse Effect?

Is the greenhouse effect the same as global warming?

No. But the greenhouse effect is key to understanding what causes global warming—it's the process by which the atmosphere holds heat around our planet. Without the greenhouse effect, the earth would be a frozen wasteland. The average surface temperature would be about 54 degrees F. (30 degrees C.) cooler than it is today—too cold to support life as we know it.

Why is it called the greenhouse effect?

Have you ever gone inside a glass greenhouse where plants are grown in the winter and noticed that the temperature is much higher inside than it is outside? What happens in a greenhouse is similar to what happens on earth. The earth has a layer of gases that act similarly to a layer of glass on a greenhouse that lets sunlight pass inside but traps heat that would otherwise be lost to space.

Here's another way to experience the greenhouse effect: On a sunny day, if your family car is parked directly in the sun with the windows rolled up, you'll notice that the temperature inside the car can be much higher than it is outside. The glass windows in the car are trapping the heat.

How does the greenhouse effect work?

Kind of the same way a sleeping bag traps your body heat when it's cold outside. Energy from the sun enters the atmosphere and passes by greenhouse gases without being affected. The sun's rays are absorbed by the earth, then reflected back at longer heat *wavelengths*. Greenhouse gases absorb some of this heat, trapping it within the lower atmosphere.

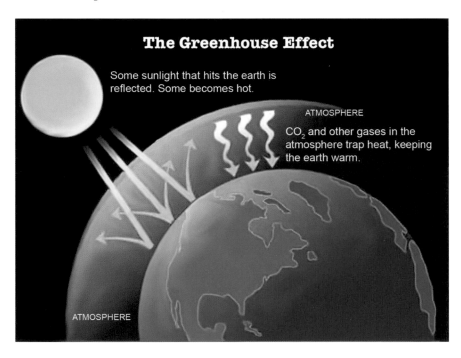

The greenhouse effect.

What are the main greenhouse gases?

Carbon dioxide (the chemical name is CO_2) is the most significant greenhouse gas directly released into the atmosphere by people. It's thought to be responsible for at least half of human-created global warming.

You might think of carbon dioxide as the stuff that makes your soda bubbly. But it's also one of the basic substances of life. People and other animals create it when we exhale, while plants use it to make leaves and flowers. As animals and plants disintegrate, they release carbon dioxide again. When coal and other fossil fuels are burned or trees are cut down, carbon dioxide is also released.

A Carbon Dioxide Molecule

The chemical structure of carbon dioxide—two oxygen atoms and one carbon atom.

Methane, another important greenhouse gas, is the main chemical in natural gas. It's also produced when organic matter decays; that occurs in places like landfills containing rotting garbage and the swampy paddies where rice is grown. Methane is produced by farm animals when they digest food.

Methane isn't as abundant as carbon dioxide but is at least 20 times more effective at absorbing heat and re-radiating it back to the earth. It's considered responsible for about one-fourth of human-caused global warming.

Nitrous oxide (also known as laughing gas) comes out of car and truck tailpipes and is produced in some fertilizers used for agriculture. Although it's responsible for only about 6 percent of human-caused global warming, it's much more powerful than carbon dioxide as a greenhouse gas, and it can stay in the atmosphere for more than a century.

Cows grazing.

What are the other greenhouse gases?

The many other greenhouse gases are present in very small amounts. They include chlorofluorocarbons (CFCs), which are chemicals used in refrigerators and air conditioners. They contribute only slightly to global warming but are a main contributor to the *ozone hole* in the atmosphere.

Is water vapor in the atmosphere a greenhouse gas?

Actually, it's the most abundant one. But its effects are very short lived. Water vapor only stays in the atmosphere for a short time—like a few days—before it falls as rain or snow. Meanwhile, heat-trapping emissions from human sources can have a very long life in the atmosphere, so they keep accumulating.

Also, the more the atmosphere warms, the more water vapor it can hold, which in turn causes the atmosphere to warm more.

Is smog a greenhouse gas?

No. Smog (which comes from combining the words "smoke" and "fog") is the hazy pollution that you see blanketing big cities. It's made up of nitrogen oxides and volatile organic compounds that are mainly coughed up by the tailpipe emissions from cars and other sources like factories. But scientists do warn that the warmer temperatures from rapid global warming will create more smog.

Smog.

Are the ozone hole and global warming related?

The ozone hole is a different phenomenon than global warming, but there are some links between them. It's not an actual hole in the sky but an area of the atmosphere where ozone levels are lower than expected.

On the ground, ozone is unhealthy to people—it's a big health risk to people with asthma and other lung problems. But in the upper atmosphere, the ozone layer acts as a shield to protect the earth's people, animals, and plant life from the sun's ultraviolet (UV) radiation.

The ozone hole refers to the loss of ozone in the stratosphere, one of the higher levels of the earth's atmosphere. This is a big concern because stratospheric ozone blocks incoming ultraviolet radiation from the sun, some of which is harmful to plants, humans, and animals.

Ozone loss was recognized as a big threat in the 1980s. Scientists' observations led to an agreement called the Montreal Protocol on Substances That Deplete the Ozone Layer. The protocol is a 160-nation international treaty that came into effect in 1989. It phased out the production of ozone-depleting CFCs and other substances in industrialized countries.

The treaty helped lead to a sharp decline in these ozone-depleting gases. Many people who want to fight global warming regard the Montreal Protocol as proof that if many countries take action on a scientific problem, success is possible.

How long have we known about the greenhouse effect?

A long time. In 1827, French scientist Jean-Baptiste Fourier first recognized the greenhouse effect when he compared the atmosphere to a glass vessel. He saw that some of the gases in our atmosphere act like a greenhouse because they let in sunlight but prevent some of the sun's warmth from radiating back into space.

Several decades later, Britain's John Tyndall took the next step. Tyndall measured the heat-trapping ability of various gases and was surprised by the results. Although nitrogen and oxygen are the most common gases in the atmosphere, they have no heat-trapping ability at all. He concluded that the job of warming the planet fell to other gases.

In 1896, Sweden's Svante Arrhenius calculated the effects of an increasing concentration of greenhouse gases. He was the first scientist to see the significance of what Fourier and Tyndall had theorized. Arrhenius predicted that burning fossil fuels like coal would cause global temperatures to rise. "We are evaporating our coal mines into the air," he wrote.

Then, in the late 1930s, British coal engineer George Callendar put together several decades' worth of temperatures taken at weather stations and from shipboard decks. He was the first to calculate the warming due to the increasing carbon dioxide from the burning of fossil fuels. He had a hard time getting attention for his findings—right after he came out with his results, Europe suffered a major cold spell. But his work led scientists to conduct more detailed studies so that we could learn what we know today about the greenhouse effect.

Do other planets have a greenhouse effect?

Yes. A greenhouse effect occurs on Venus, our nearest neighbor among the planets and about the same size as the earth. Venus's temperature is very hot—almost 1,000 degrees F. (538 degrees C.)—and the atmosphere is heavy with carbon dioxide. Only a very strong greenhouse effect can account for Venus's high temperatures.

Venus.

Mars, on the other hand, also has a lot of carbon dioxide, but its atmosphere is very thin and so the greenhouse effect is small. Mars has barely any water vapor in its atmosphere to help trap the sun's heat. As a result, Mars's temperature is more than 50 degrees F. below zero (minus 46 degrees C.), colder than Antarctica.

So if the greenhouse effect is a natural thing, then what's the problem?

The problem is that the balance of greenhouse gases in the atmosphere is being upset because of human activity. That's causing warmer temperatures that lead to changes in climate. And that, in turn, causes the problems people refer to when they talk about global warming. We'll discuss that in the next chapter.

The Greenhouse Effect in a Jar

Here's a simple experiment that allows you to see for yourself the effect of a greenhouse. You will need:

2 small thermometers
1 jar or other see-through container
1 clock or watch
1 worksheet
Access to a sunny area or a sunlamp to perform the experiment

Place the thermometers a few inches apart under the sunlamp or in direct sunlight.

Wait about three minutes so that the thermometers will give accurate readings. Then record the temperature readings on both thermometers as well as the time.

Place the jar over one of the thermometers, taking care that it doesn't cast a shadow over the uncovered one. (If the thermometers are too large to stay horizontal inside the jars, stand them against an inner side.) Every minute, for 10 minutes, record the readings of both thermometers.

What's happening: The air over the exposed thermometer is constantly changing, and as it gets warm, it's replaced by cooler air. Because the air in the jar can't circulate to the rest of the room, this air stays in the sunlight, getting warmer and warmer.

A similar trapping of heat happens in the earth's atmosphere. Sunlight passes through the atmosphere and warms the earth's surface. The heat radiating from the surface is trapped by greenhouse gases.

ACTIVITY

CHAPTER 3

How Are People Affecting the Climate?

How are people changing the climate?

By altering the natural system known as the carbon cycle. Carbon is a chemical element found everywhere on the earth. There's about a trillion tons of it around us, and the amount lying underground is much, much greater. Carbon bonds with almost everything that isn't made of metal. About one-fifth of your body is made of carbon.

Carbon is introduced into the atmosphere as carbon dioxide—the most important greenhouse gas. This can happen in

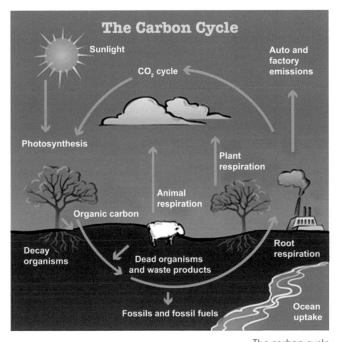

The carbon cycle.

any number of ways. Volcanoes, for example, can bring up carbon dioxide and other gases when they erupt.

Carbon is constantly shifting in and out of our bodies, as well as from rocks to sea or soils and to the atmosphere and back again. People and animals contribute to the carbon cycle when they breathe in oxygen, combine it with the carbon in their bodies, and breathe it out as carbon dioxide. Its movements are based on various factors, like the temperature and our activities.

Much of the carbon released into the air is recycled by the oceans and in trees and other plants, which pull carbon out of the atmosphere. It's released again when they die and decay, forming a cycle.

How are human activities changing the carbon cycle?

When humans use more carbon-based fuels—oil, coal, and natural gas—or burn and cut down the world's forests, it puts more carbon dioxide in the air while impairing nature's ability to take excess carbon out of the air.

As the population has grown, demand for fossil fuels has increased. Ten thousand years ago, only about 10 million people were living on the earth. Today, almost that many live in and around Chicago.

The average American generates, through all their activities, about 10 tons (11 metric tons) of carbon dioxide emissions per year. That's his or her *carbon footprint*. But that number doesn't account for all the extra energy needed to produce goods, like clothing and food, that people buy. If those factors are considered, each person's carbon footprint is slightly more than 20 tons (22 metric tons).

Overall, scientists have concluded, the impact of people on climate over the last two centuries has greatly exceeded the impacts from natural changes like volcanoes erupting. The United States is responsible for about one-quarter of global greenhouse gas emissions to date—and its emissions are continuing to increase.

When did people start affecting the climate?

You might think it was when they started driving cars and building factories, but it actually began when humans started farming and ranching. The removal of trees in forests and the tilling of land for agriculture produce about one-quarter of the greenhouse gases released by humans into the atmosphere.

Carbon is extremely important to forests. Plants absorb carbon dioxide, convert it to food and energy, and release oxygen into the atmosphere. Forests also act as carbon *sinks*, or places where carbon is stored. Forests often have been cleared by burning, which can be faster than cutting. When trees are burned, the carbon stored in

Carbon is important to forests.

their leaves and trunks gets released. Some carbon also is released when trees are cut or fall and start to decompose.

Forests once covered much of the earth but have been reduced by as much as half. In the United States, all but 6 percent of the original forest cover has been cleared. It's only in the last 100 years or so that people have been seriously interested in saving them.

More recently, activists have sought to preserve *old-growth* forests—those never logged whose trees are at least 150 years old. The activists say these trees are needed to protect many animal species, like the *endangered* spotted owl.

What else has been happening in forests?

Recently the destruction of the tropical rain forest has been in the news, not just for its effects on climate but for the many kinds of plants and animals that are being wiped out by development. Rain forests are usually found near the sea or in mountainous regions that get a lot of rain.

The largest rain forests are found in the Amazon Basin of South America, in West African countries that skirt the equator, and in South Pacific countries like Indonesia and the Philippines. Smaller tracts of rain forests exist throughout Central America, parts of Mexico and Hawaii, and other islands of the Pacific and Caribbean.

The burning of rain forests has contributed to global warming.

Circling the earth's equator like a belt, the tropical rain forests maintain a near constant temperature of 80 degrees F. (27 degrees C.) and receive anywhere from 160 to 400 inches (406 to 1,016 centimeters) of rain per year. Such favorable weather conditions allow a large number of species to flourish year-round. The tropical rain forests were spared the great loss of life that occurred on other parts of the earth during the ice ages. The heavy rainfall and the fact that life wasn't wiped

out during the ice ages help explain why the tropical rain forests are home to between 50 and 70 million different life forms.

The rain forests have been disappearing in recent years at a rate of around four acres (1.6 hectares)—that's two football fields—every second. That's more than twice the size of Florida every year. Because of all the burning done in forests, massive amounts of carbon dioxide are released into the atmosphere. All of that burning has led Brazil to be ranked among the world's worst contributors to global warming, even though the country has relatively little industry.

What about farming?

Farming affects the climate in a number ways, like the plowing of fields. Deep plowing allows more oxygen into the soil, speeding up the decay of organic matter and the release of carbon dioxide.

Animals—particularly cows—also are responsible. More than a billion cattle are now roaming the earth. Cows produce methane when bacteria breaks down cellulose in their stomachs, releasing gas. Most of the methane comes out through their mouths. (Scientists in Canada and Sweden have actually mea-sured how much gas is released when cows belch.)

Rice paddies also contribute to global warming.

And then there's rice, an important crop for much of the world. Methane emissions from rice paddies have been shown to be a main contributor to all greenhouse gases during the last century.

A rice paddy is a plain of land that is flooded so its roots can make use of the *nutrient* content of the water it was planted in. Paddy rice farmers usually plant the seeds first in little seedbeds and transfer them into flooded fields that already have been plowed.

The bacteria that thrive in flooded rice paddies produce methane by decomposing manure used as fertilizer. "There is no other crop that is emitting such a large amount of greenhouse gases," Reiner Wassmann, a climate change specialist at the International Rice Research Institute in the Philippines, told the Associated Press.

Factories increase emissions into the atmosphere.

What about industry?

The creation of machines and tools has made our lives easier, but it's definitely changed the atmosphere.

The change to machines and tools began during the Industrial Revolution, which started back in the 1700s, when British kings and queens became more interested in trading goods with other countries and built *waterways* to ship those goods. The British textile industry was looking for ways to speed up the process of making clothes.

James Watt, a Scottish engineer, invented the steam engine in the 1760s. That invention fueled the revolution. More inventions followed, including steam-powered trains and boats and large factories devoted to producing steel. Eventually the revolution spread throughout Europe, the United States, and Asia. Factories began sprouting up everywhere.

As the Industrial Revolution continued and the world's population grew, more energy was needed. Steel, glass, aluminum, and cement all became important in constructing buildings, roads, and other things—but all required the burning of massive amounts of fossil fuels, which release carbon dioxide. Since the start of the Industrial Revolution, the amount of carbon dioxide has risen from 277 *parts per million* to 387 parts per million (in 2009).

What about cars?

Cars were a part of the shift toward oil as the world's important energy source. The first cars started appearing in the late 1890s. Within a couple of decades, Henry Ford began the modern assembly line to make cars quickly and cheaply, and they became much more common.

As cars became an essential part of every household and as the highway system developed, they became a major source of greenhouse gas emissions. Every gallon of gasoline that's consumed produces about five pounds (2.3 kilograms) of carbon. (When you measure carbon dioxide emissions, it's the weight of the carbon that matters.) The average car creates, over its lifetime, about 70 tons (77 metric tons) of carbon dioxide. The average sport-utility vehicle creates around 100 tons (110 metric tons).

Here's another statistic: just the cars and trucks in the United States emit more carbon dioxide than the total output—that's the *entire* output—of all but three other countries (China, Russia, and Japan).

Cars are a major greenhouse gas emissions source.

Didn't anyone see the link to climate change years ago?

Yes. Swedish chemist Svante Arrhenius recognized in the late 1890s and early 1900s that industrialization and climate change were closely related and that the consumption of fossil fuels would lead to more warming. But Arrhenius thought the buildup of carbon dioxide in the air would be very slow, partly because he thought the oceans would act as a sort of sponge that could soak up extra carbon dioxide.

After he died in 1927, interest in the subject also died. But then in the mid-1950s, young chemist Charles David Keeling convinced the U.S. Weather Bureau to let him start measuring carbon dioxide every year from Hawaii's Mount Mauna Loa, 11,000 feet (3,350 meters) above sea level.

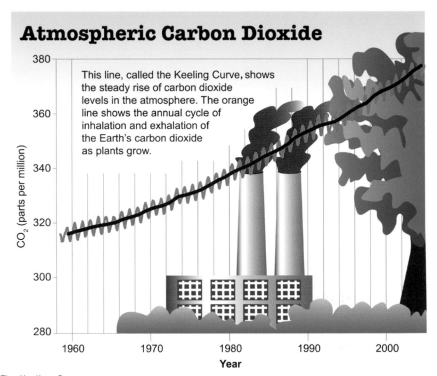

The Keeling Curve.

What did Keeling find?

Carbon dioxide levels rise and fall over the course of a day, and Keeling's first measurement at Mauna Loa showed an average concentration of 315 parts per million. By 1970, that measurement reached 325 parts per million, and by 1990, it was up to 354 parts per million.

Keeling's measurements also showed that carbon dioxide levels rise and fall with the seasons. In all, his work had a dramatic impact on climate change science. His graph has become one of the most famous figures in all of science.

Due in part to the significance of Keeling's findings, the U.S. government began monitoring carbon dioxide levels all over the world in the 1970s. Today, CO_2 levels are checked at more than 100 sites worldwide.

What else has happened in recent decades to affect the climate?

The use of coal for electricity generation has increased. You might think of coal as those black lumps of charcoal you use on the barbecue grill (which are actually made from sawdust and other wood by-products that are burned and compressed with ground coal), but coal is an important fuel. In the United States, coal provides around half of our electric power, and it accounts for more than 90 percent of the carbon dioxide emissions from the companies that produce electricity.

Coal is an abundant resource here as well as in many other countries. Power plants that use it are cheaper to operate than those that run on other sources of energy. But when coal gets burned, it emits more than 1.5 times as much carbon per unit of energy as natural gas and 1.25 times as much as oil.

Coal is an important electricity source, but it contributes to global warming.

So why don't we just stop building coal plants?

Because people keep using electricity. The coal industry says new plants are needed over the next few years to meet rising demand and replace aging, less efficient plants. About 90 percent of U.S. coal plants are more than 20 years old.

What other ways does using electricity increase global warming?

From many different activities. For example, if you keep your lights on at home (three lights for six hours a day), that generates about 1.5 pounds (0.7 kilogram) of carbon dioxide. Even simply taking a bath generates as much as 3.5 pounds (1.6 kilograms), based on the energy required to pump the water to your house and heat it up. (Showers generally use less.)

What other activities cause climate change?

The rapid growth of air travel has been a cause of climate change. Emissions from the fuel used by jets and water vapor emissions from their exhausts both contribute to climate change in special ways. These greenhouse gases are emitted at high altitudes, where few other gases are present.

Planes emit contrails as exhaust when they fly.

Also, the emissions form ice crystals in aviation contrails—those cloud-like streams of condensation you see behind planes in the sky. The contrails can produce more clouds that have a cooling or warming effect, depending on the shape and makeup of the ice crystals. Most scientists believe that the overall effect of contrails is warming.

The Intergovernmental Panel on Climate Change has said aviation causes only about 3.5 percent of global warming, but the panel has predicted that figure could rise as high as 15 percent by 2050 as air travel increases.

What are some of the factors that will influence how much greenhouse gas is generated in the future?

One is how many people will be on the earth. Estimates for 2050 range from 7.4 billion to 10.6 billion. (Right now, the population is

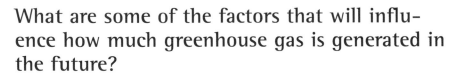

a little less than 7 billion.) Another factor is how much economic growth occurs: will factories and other businesses increase demand for fossil fuels?

All those people will have to eat. An International Solid Waste Foundation study predicted in 2006 that by 2025, food waste could go up by 44 percent worldwide. When food waste rots, it releases methane, a greenhouse gas. The Environmental Protection Agency (EPA) has estimated that landfills account for more than one-third of all methane emissions in the United States.

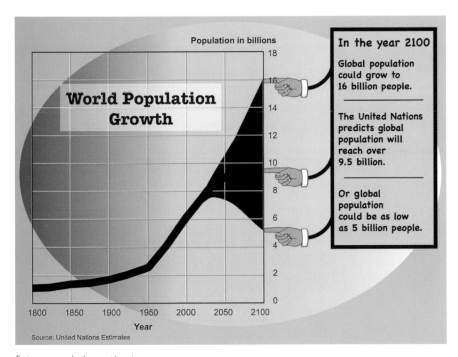

Future population estimates.

The rate at which new technologies are adopted is also a factor in the increase of greenhouse gas emissions. If countries with rapid population growth like China use the latest and most energy-efficient technologies, less carbon dioxide will be produced than if they use less efficient—but often cheaper—technologies.

Calculating Greenhouse Gas Emissions

Find the EPA greenhouse gas emissions personal calculator online at http://epa.gov/climatechange/emissions/ind_calculator.html. Use it to calculate your own personal greenhouse gas emissions. What range are you in? Are you above or below the average American? In what specific areas?

ACTIVITY

CHAPTER 4

What Could Happen If Global Warming Doesn't Stop?

What's going to happen from climate change?

It depends on where you live. The impacts won't be the same everywhere. But in the future, a warmer climate could be a factor in everything from:

How many more birds you see in your backyard (birds like the bobwhite and field sparrow are dying in greater numbers as climate change interferes with their regular migration schedules).

How much guacamole will cost you (California's avocado production is expected to drop by as much as 40 percent over the next 40 years).

How many mosquitoes bite you (dry spells caused by hotter weather will reduce populations of the dragonflies and frogs that eat mosquitoes).

How often you get poison ivy (the vine grows faster and bigger as carbon dioxide levels in the atmosphere rise—and also produces more of its rash-causing chemical).

Many more damaging effects may result from global warming. It might harm plants and animals that live in the sea, and it could force animals and plants on land to seek new areas where they can more easily find food. In certain parts of the world, disease could spread and farmers could harvest fewer crops.

Weather patterns will change, but in an uneven way. Some parts of the world are going to get a little hotter, while others will be much, much hotter. (Some places may initially be a little cooler, depending on the winds or ocean currents.) Temperatures at the center of continents will warm faster than land near the oceans.

Penguins on a small iceberg off the Antarctic Peninsula.

The Intergovernmental Panel on Climate Change—the scientists from many countries studying the problem—says the earth will warm an average of between 2.0 and 11.5 degrees F. (1.1 and 6.4 degrees C.) by 2100. That's a big range, but it's hard to pinpoint future greenhouse gas emissions and how the climate will respond.

But here's one example: by 2080, if global warming continues unchecked, planners in Chicago worry that their city's climate could be roughly the same as that of Houston, Texas.

A warmer climate can lead to extreme weather—heat waves, storms, hurricanes, and drought. But it's very important to know that *no* single extreme weather event—including Hurricane Katrina—can be directly blamed on global warming. Those events might have happened anyway. Instead, scientists strongly believe a warmer climate makes such events more *likely*.

It's also very important to keep in mind that the people most responsible for a changing climate (countries like the United States with lots of industries and cars giving off carbon dioxide) won't suffer as much as people in other, less populous places (poorer countries with less industry and more agriculture).

Why is that?

Big, modern industrialized countries like the United States are better able to cope with climate change:

They're in parts of the world with climates that are lucky to be neither too hot nor too cold. In other words, they're not in the tropics or the Arctic.

They have rich soil that can grow many different crops over a long and generous growing season.

And they have a lot of money. That helps sustain an economy with lots of different businesses. Money also helps keep people well fed and healthy. It funds inventions to eliminate or reduce climate change's effects.

That means the United States, where agriculture is responsible for only a small percentage of the overall economy, can cope with climate change much better than a country like Malawi, a tiny, poor republic in southeast Africa, where most of the people live in rural areas and agriculture drives 40 percent of the economy.

A government official in Malawi pointed out to the *New York Times* in 2007 that he has no money to help learn how much climate change is happening. He said people in his country can't fix broken and outdated equipment to make accurate measurements: "We cannot even know the duration of sunshine in our country for four years, so how can we measure climate change?"

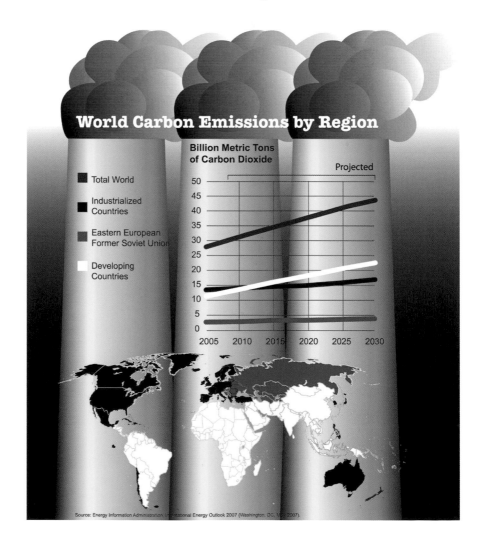

Why should we care?

Because climate change is going to hit places like this harder than the United States, that could make it harder for the world to take action in a unified way. Already, planners in the military have raised concerns that climate change in poor countries could contribute to poverty, rioting, and wars. These planners want the government to start thinking about how to be ready to respond.

Religious groups are concerned, too. The National Council of Churches, which represents 45 million members nationwide, said in a 2008 report that faith organizations will need to increase humanitarian funding by six times their current budgets to resettle refugees because of the expected impacts of climate change. Such groups also would have to double the amount of food they provide to developing countries.

Why is there so much talk about the North Pole and global warming?

The Arctic (where the North Pole is) was the first place to noticeably show the effects of global warming. It provides a warning of what could happen elsewhere. Predictions are that the Arctic will warm more than other places.

The Arctic is warming more because of its albedo (how reflective a surface is) and temperature. In the summer, when sea ice melts, the surface of the water is darker than it is the rest of the year and soaks up more solar radiation, which speeds up warming. This is also true for countries in the area like Greenland and northern Canada. On average, climate warming in these regions is two or three times greater than anywhere else.

Opposite: Past and future carbon emissions.

Why is climate warming in the Arctic important?

What happens in the polar regions matters for the rest of the world. Faster melting there means the sea level will eventually rise and lead to faster changes in winter weather.

Sea ice in the Arctic has been shrinking in all seasons, most dramatically in the summer. In recent years, it has shrunk at a much faster rate than scientists thought possible. Some of them were extremely surprised and said they believe the ice there could disappear entirely by 2040.

And there have been dramatic reductions in the permafrost—the frozen soil found in the Arctic regions whose age is thought to go back thousands of years.

The ice in the permafrost helps maintain the structure of the soil. When it melts, trees can start to fall or sinkholes can develop that can fill up with water and kill trees. Thawed permafrost can release its carbon as methane, a key greenhouse gas.

Is the same thing happening at the South Pole?

The two places are different. The ice at the South Pole (Antarctica) can be two miles (3.2 kilometers) thick, while the North Pole ice floats on seawater and is only a few feet (about a meter) thick, so it melts more easily. Antarctica's ice sheet, which covers the continent, is actually two sheets. The larger one is old and not considered likely to melt in the near future, but the smaller one is more vulnerable, and scientists are studying it to try to predict its future.

Some areas of the Antarctic have gotten cooler in recent decades. That's because circular winds around the continent have become stronger and prevent warmer air from reaching its interior.

Skeptics of global warming say this is evidence that the world isn't warming up. But scientists say that what's important is the

Arctic Sea Ice Retreat

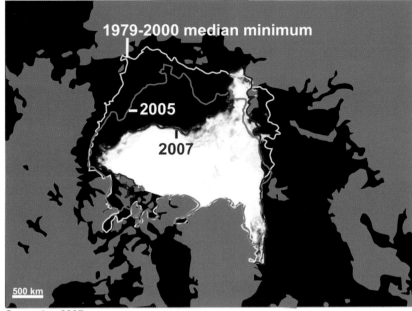

1979-2000 median minimum

2005

2007

500 km

September 2007

Sea Ice Concentration

Arctic sea ice retreat.

overall picture and that far more areas of the world are warming than cooling.

What about the United States?

Again, the effects of global warming will depend on where you live. Here's what could happen in some states:

Alaska: Because of its size and location far away from the continental United States, Alaska has its own specific problems from climate change. Most of the United States is projected to have greater warming in summer than in winter, but Alaska experiences far more warming in winter than summer.

In the last 50 years, its temperature has gone up 5.5 degrees F. (3.1 degrees C.)—twice the rate of increase of the rest of the world. By 2100, under current projections, average temperatures are expected to go up anywhere between five and 18 degrees F. (2.8 and 10 degrees C.). Its forests will be damaged by warming and pest outbreaks— higher summer temperatures in 2004 brought about a record year for forest fires and burned an area the size of New Hampshire.

A reduction in sea ice will disrupt the habits of polar bears and other wildlife. Melting permafrost will cause sinking and tilting buildings and roads, falling electricity poles, and broken underground pipelines. With many of the state's people living near its coastline, the threat of flooding of low-lying property and beach erosion will increase. Some Native Alaskan villages could be forced to move, which will cost a lot of money.

California: With 38 million residents and counting, California has more people than any other state—and also has its own problems from climate change.

Scientists have estimated that if global heat-trapping emissions continue at a medium to high rate, temperatures are expected to rise 4.7 to 10.5 degrees F. (2.6 to 5.8 degrees C.) by the end of the century. Even a lower emissions rate would result in a temperature rise between three and 5.6 degrees F. (1.7 and 3.1 degrees C.). These temperature increases would reduce the snow in the mountains that feeds rivers and provides water, increase the risk of large wildfires, and reduce what kinds of crops are grown (like the avocados mentioned earlier).

California, which already has the country's worst air quality, could have many more days in which the weather causes air pollution. And as many as 100 additional days a year could have temperatures above 90 degrees F. (32 degrees C.) in Los Angeles and above 95 degrees F. (35 degrees C.) in Sacramento, in the northern part of the state.

Florida: As the southernmost state and surrounded largely by water, Florida is another place with special problems. If nothing is done, one 2008 study predicted, a temperature increase of as much as 10 degrees F. (5.6 degrees C.) is possible by 2100. The daily highs in many cities will be more than 90 degrees F. (32 degrees C.) for almost two-thirds of the year.

Rainfall might be lower, severe hurricanes could increase, and the sea might rise by more than three feet (one meter)—which would affect more than 1.5 million people. (More about sea level rise later in this chapter.) Beaches could shrink or disappear, affecting the state's tourism industry and causing significant harm to the economy.

Louisiana: Louisiana is already losing 25 to 50 square miles (65 to 130 square kilometers) of its land a year to erosion. If the climate keeps changing at its current rate, 70 percent of Louisiana's remaining coastal wetlands—low-lying areas either regularly or permanently covered with water—will be gone by the end of the century, endangering the state bird, the brown pelican, and many other species. The international climate change panel listed New Orleans as North America's most vulnerable city to the impacts of climate change because of its low elevation, its disappearance of land, and its vulnerability to future hurricanes.

Flooding in Louisiana following Hurricane Katrina.

All of this will affect the productivity of the state's fishing industry. And as in other areas, the risk of forest fires will increase: climate models predict that because of climate change, the entire southeastern United States will have a 30 percent greater chance of risk of forest fires by the middle of this century.

Massachusetts: Beaches, sand dunes, and marshes along Massachusetts' coast provide homes for many plants and animals. Not all will be able to adapt to eroding shorelines and saltwater infiltrating low-lying freshwater areas. Other plants and animals, like the sugar maple tree, will move farther north as temperatures get warmer and could eventually disappear from the state.

Popular seafood like lobster and scallops will become more susceptible to disease because of rising temperatures. Coastlines will erode, and the risk of flooding from rising sea levels will increase. Those floods will put a strain on how well bridges and roads function. Ski areas in Massachusetts (and nearby states like Maine and Vermont) will get less snow too.

Michigan: Reduced snowfall and higher temperatures from climate change will increase the risk of drought in Michigan. In a long drought, even deep-rooted trees can dry up and plants can take years to recover. Temperatures could be much more like those in southern Missouri, Kentucky, or northern Arkansas in the next century.

With more heat, there's less ice and more evaporation, which could cause water levels in the Great Lakes to decline. The evaporation is likely to lower lake levels by as much as three feet (one meter) in the next 50 years. That would harm the recreation and shipping industries. The numbers of some popular types of fish found in lakes, like yellow perch and northern pike, could drop as temperatures rise.

New York: Temperatures are expected to go up by as much as five degrees F. (2.3 degrees C.) by 2100. As in other states, that will contribute to problems due to rising sea levels as well as a greater risk of forest fires.

Dairy farmers (New York is the nation's fifth-largest dairy producer) will have to spend more money on food and water to keep their cows producing milk. And the higher temperatures will make problems like air pollution worse, causing trouble for people with asthma. Because the New York City area is so densely populated, heat waves could be more frequent and intense, causing more deaths.

What will happen with heat waves in the rest of the country?

The number of heat waves (several days or weeks of unusually hot weather, often with high humidity) has gone up in the last few decades. Extremely hot days (with temperatures in the 90s and 100s F.; 50s C.) have become more frequent, and scientists say more such days are to come. That could mean more illness and death, especially for elderly and poor people in cities like Chicago (where a 1995 heat wave left more than 700 people dead) who don't have ways to get air conditioning.

The asphalt, concrete, brick, and glass in cities all soak up and hold heat, causing buildings made of those materials to bake like ovens. Heat also releases pollen, mold, and other triggers of allergies. And it contributes to air pollution. One study found that people living in cities across the East are expected to see twice as many "red alert" air pollution days caused by higher temperatures from climate change.

But it's important to know that extreme events usually can be caused by a combination of factors—and that scientists don't regard global warming as the only cause of heat waves.

Is climate change making hurricanes worse?

Climate change doesn't create hurricanes. But some scientists believe it contributes to making them stronger and more dangerous.

Because the ocean is getting warmer, tropical storms can pick up more energy and become more powerful, so a storm could become much more dangerous. In fact, scientists have found that the destructive potential of hurricanes has greatly increased along with ocean temperature over the past few decades. But many scientists say the link between hurricanes and climate change needs more study.

Even if there aren't more hurricanes, will there be more rain?

Because of the uncertainties of local weather, it's very difficult to estimate how much precipitation, including rain and snow, will change in a specific place. In general, areas in higher latitudes, closer to the poles, and oceans may get more, while areas in lower latitudes, closer to the equator, and farther inland may get less.

But because of climate change, there may be more periods of very heavy rain. These extreme rains cause flooding and erosion, putting a big burden on flood insurance systems. This is expected to happen more often in Northeastern and Midwestern states.

What about places that get less rain?

If the rainfall is low for long periods, like a number of years, the ecosystem turns into desert, making it impossible for any grasses or trees to find water. The International Panel on Climate Change is concerned that water shortages could affect the western United States as well as parts of Africa, Brazil, and countries around the Mediterranean Sea.

Some popular fruits and vegetables—apples, blueberries, strawberries, grapes, cucumbers, asparagus, celery, tomatoes, beans, and carrots—could become more vulnerable as their growing patterns have trouble adjusting to warmer temperatures. Farmers will end up having to change what kinds of crops they grow—and in some poor countries, food shortages could occur due to ongoing drought.

What about snow?

There's been a global decline in snow and ice that has been especially extreme since 1980. The snow that covers mountains is retreating earlier in the spring, and the *snowpack* (the total amount of snow and ice on the ground) in the western United States could go down by 70 percent by the middle of this century.

In many areas, snow and ice masses are big sources of irrigation and drinking water. In the southwestern United States, for example, the Colorado River depends on the snowfields of the Rockies for much of its flow. With less snow, there's less water for farms and homes.

Climate experts say snowfall is harder to predict than rain because it depends on a broader range of factors, like the temperature in the atmosphere. Some climate models show that big blizzards could happen in places like Chicago up until around 2040. But in the decades after that, the models show, the climate starts to become too warm to have much snow.

What about glaciers?

The melting of glaciers—massive rivers of ice formed from compacted layers of snow—is one of the most visible signs of climate change. Nearly every major glacier in the world has been shrinking in recent years.

In Montana's Glacier National Park, the number of glaciers has dropped since 1850 from 150 to fewer than 30. Some worry that none will be left within 30 years. And in the Swiss Alps, melting glaciers caused a rock the size of two Empire State Buildings to collapse 700 feet (213 meters) onto a canyon floor.

The South American country of Peru is especially concerned about melting glaciers. One giant glacier is melting 10 times more rapidly than it was in the 1960s. Many of Peru's farmers irrigate their wheat and potatoes with river water from melted glaciers, putting

Grinnell Glacier 1850-1981

1850

1968   1937

1981

A 1981 aerial photograph of Grinnell Glacier in Glacier National Park shows its retreat since 1850.

the country's food supply in danger. Other countries that depend on glaciers for drinking water—like India and China, which get water from the Himalayas—could also be at risk.

What about the oceans?

Even though land warms more than oceans, the seas are also getting warmer. Water warms at the surface and gradually mixes with deeper water, so the deeper you go, the less warming has occurred.

Warm sea temperatures affect the fish and plants living in the water. Warmer water has lots of plankton (microscopic plants and animals) for fish to eat. But if the water gets too warm, it can kill the plankton, making the fish that do survive smaller and affecting their ability to reproduce.

Warming sea temperatures also threaten coral reefs, the fragile underwater gardens that are home to millions of different kinds of marine plants and animals. Scientists have found that rapid rises in carbon dioxide cause ocean water to become more acidic, which makes it harder for coral reefs to form and makes them more suscep-tible to storm damage. A study in 2007 found that levels of carbon dioxide could kill off all coral reefs in as little as 50 years from now.

All of these effects could hurt not only the plants and animals but the economies of places like Australia, which depends on tourists coming to see the famous Great Barrier Reef.

Warmer ocean waters also lead to rising sea levels. Global warm-ing isn't the only reason for sea-level rise, but it's likely to make the impacts of other environmental problems (for example, soil erosion) even worse.

A partially bleached coral. In recent decades, coral bleaching has become more common as a result of increasing ocean temperatures associated with global warming.

Why would sea levels rise if the climate gets warmer?

Oceans absorb heat from the atmosphere. As the atmosphere warms, the oceans do too. When water warms, it expands, causing sea levels to go up. This happens gradually over years and years—you're not going to suddenly see the water surge up like it was filling a bathtub. But sea levels still rise faster than scientists would like. A rise of a few inches might not sound like much, but the rise isn't uniform—in some places, it will be higher and in a few places lower.

Also, as the temperature of the oceans and atmosphere increases, it leads to more melting of glaciers and ice sheets, which releases water into the oceans.

Why is this a big deal?

About half the world's people live near coasts. Even a few inches' rise in sea level can add a lot to their problems. Low-lying small islands

Golden toad.

will also lose land. When big storms happen, they can cause surges that bring sea flooding to land.

Countries like the Netherlands (often called Holland) that sit largely below sea level will have to spend lots of money to ensure they're protected against the sea getting too high and causing floods. In Bangladesh, a poor country in southern Asia, the three-foot (one-meter) sea level rise that is predicted if no action is taken will eventually flood more than 15 percent of the entire country. That affects more than 13 million people.

What will happen to animals?

Climate change will change the patterns of where plants grow. When that happens, the wild animals that feed on plants will try to keep up. But some will do better than others.

You may have heard about what's happening with polar bears due to the loss of their sea-ice home in the Arctic. The bears use the sea ice as their springboard into the ocean to hunt seals as food. With fewer months of solid ice, the bears' hunting season has been shortened—some bears have even resorted to cannibalism in order to survive. The U.S. Geological Survey has predicted that if the sea ice continues to melt early, two-thirds of the world's polar bears could die in 50 years.

But the polar bear isn't the only animal at risk. Frogs, penguins, butterflies, and other animals are all threatened because they are expected to have trouble adapting to climate change quickly enough.

The golden toad of Costa Rica is the first creature whose extinction is believed to have been caused by climate change. This toad used to live in the misty, humid forests of Costa Rica, but the growing heat affected the toad's moist, breathing skin, and people stopped seeing the toad in the late 1980s.

Other species have likely become extinct from climate change, but those extinctions haven't been recorded yet. "Even when animals don't go extinct, we're affecting them," David Skelly, a Yale University professor, told the *Washington Post*. Climate change causes ripples in the *food web* when certain species move to new areas. That can upset the balance between species, and some animals will have trouble adjusting.

Won't *anything* good come from climate change?

When it gets warmer in very cold places, the demand for energy for heat is less. Because of the loss of sea ice, the Arctic Ocean could be open for more ships, which could bring more business and tourism to some countries.

Throughout history, more people have died of exposure to cold weather than to hot weather. So the overall number of weather-related deaths might go down in the future.

Farmers in northern states and Canada could harvest crops that are hardy enough to adjust to warm weather. Forests could expand (if they don't burn first) and provide more wood. Some types of fish, like bass and bluegill, could thrive as temperatures warm.

Retreating ice could open the way for more oil drilling in Greenland—which is a good or bad thing, depending on how you look at our dependence on oil. Canada, Russia, and other places could get more tourists, who wouldn't otherwise come in colder weather.

But in the end, climate change won't give any big benefits.

A longer growing season does a farmer no good if resulting rain patterns bring drought. People saving on winter heating fuel might just have to spend more on air conditioning in the summer. And tourists may come to Canada, but what if lower lake levels mean that ships can't get into Canada's ports?

The changes affecting plants and animals from climate change are irreversible for the planet, while saving a little money on heating in winter is a small economic gain for some people.

So keep in mind that climate change is expected to do far more harm than good. The problem isn't just that climate change is occurring—it's that climate change is happening far more suddenly and rapidly than ever before.

How Will Your Area Be Affected By Global Warming?

Look at the geography of where you live. Are you in a big city, a suburb, or a rural area? On or near a river or an ocean? Near a desert or forests? Make a list of all the things that you think could be impacted by climate change and its effects.

Also look at your area's economy. Are there lots of farms? What types of things are grown? Do many tourists visit to ski or fish? Consider how they might all be affected.

ACTIVITY

What Are Politicians Doing About Global Warming?

Why aren't the people elected to government office taking climate change seriously?

Many of them are. But like many things in politics, climate change is really complicated. Issues rarely get resolved quickly in politics, especially those that stir so many emotions in people.

Lawmakers in Congress disagreed for years over whether global warming was real or not. Now that evidence has accumulated that it's real and a threat, they still disagree about how seriously to take it and—most important—what steps should be taken.

On one end of the spectrum is James Inhofe, a senator from Oklahoma. He doesn't believe humans cause climate change. When he was the head of the Senate committee responsible for environmental issues, he called it "the greatest hoax ever perpetrated on the American people." On the other end is Al Gore, the former vice president who starred in the movie *An Inconvenient Truth* and who won a Nobel Peace Prize for his work. He says climate change "has become a true planetary emergency."

Most other politicians fall in between those two views. As more scientific evidence has come to light that people are to blame for accelerating global warming, many of them—like the public—have moved closer to Gore's position.

Who are the politicians doing something about climate change?

One of the best known is Arnold Schwarzenegger. You might think of him as a movie star (he was the Terminator). But he also served as the governor of California. In 2006, he and other California politi-

cal leaders agreed to get the state's carbon dioxide emissions by 2020 back to the same levels they were 30 years earlier. "We simply must do everything in our power to slow down global warming before it is too late," Governor Schwarzenegger said.

Governor Schwarzenegger's promise is a big deal, because not only does California have more people than any other state, its economy is the sixth largest in the entire world. And when you rank the entire world's biggest carbon dioxide emitters, California ranks 12th—it emits way more carbon dioxide than most countries.

California governor Arnold Schwarzenegger.

Other important politicians have joined him in taking the issue of climate change seriously. They include Charlie Crist of Florida and Tim Pawlenty of Minnesota, both of whom saw climate change as a big threat to their respective states when they were governors. "It's hard to be a Floridian and not be sensitive to it," Governor Crist said.

So why haven't more politicians felt the same way?

Politicians' main concerns are issues that immediately affect the people they represent—wars, disasters, crime, tax bills, housing prices. Most often, they react to issues instead of doing something ahead of time. Because climate change was regarded for many years as a faraway problem—if it was considered a problem at all—many politicians just put it off.

Another reason politicians haven't done more about climate change is because it's an area in which they have to depend on scientists. Climate change isn't like a street full of potholes that politicians can see needs fixing. They don't have the training, let alone the time, to collect their own scientific information.

Even though to an overwhelming extent scientists agree about the nature and scope of the climate problem, a small group of them think otherwise. That gave the appearance of a split in the scientific world. Skeptics of climate change did their best to play up that split; they invoked scientific uncertainty as a weapon against the government taking action.

Because the efforts of these skeptics got so much attention, some politicians simply decided that there was no consensus yet in the scientific community and that they were right in delaying action.

Do politicians listen to what voters say?

Politicians often look at polls to see what's on the public's mind, and people asked in those polls say global warming is important. But when people vote in an election, they are far more likely to look at where the politician stands on the issues that directly affect the voters' pocketbook and affect families, like taxes and health care.

Who else do politicians listen to?

Politicians listen to what businesses tell them, especially since business leaders often give politicians money for their campaigns. And a number of businesses—and the *lobbyists* they hire—view climate change mainly in terms of what it will cost them. Businesses are afraid that if the government acts the wrong way, it will cause them to make less money and end up hurting the economy.

People have often expressed this view in places like Michigan, which depends on the automobile industry. This industry has been hit hard economically in the last few years, and politicians from that state have been cautious about what's proposed to cut down on emissions from cars and raise the number of miles that cars are required to get per gallon of gasoline.

But not all companies resist doing something about climate change. The U.S. Climate Action Partnership is a group of major businesses and environmental groups that together have called on the U.S. government to pass laws to significantly reduce greenhouse gas emissions. Its members include automakers like Ford and General Motors plus other big corporations like General Electric, PepsiCo, and Xerox.

Companies have joined such efforts for a variety of reasons. They consider it good for their image. It allows them to be in line with companies in Europe and other countries that have taken the issue seriously. And they think working on a solution will help ensure that the eventual outcome doesn't take them by surprise.

When did government start looking at climate change?

After World War II, the government funded many kinds of research, and some of it dealt with climate change. During the 1960s, the government created major agencies for space and science, and in the

1970s, as the public got more concerned about the environment, those agencies increasingly supported studying climate change.

But the issue wasn't made a big priority. In the U.S. government, climate research has been split among a variety of agencies, including NASA and the National Oceanic and Atmospheric Administration (NOAA). (You probably think of NASA as the organization that sends astronauts into space, but it's also the main agency for launching satellites that collect information on climate change.)

The science of climate change has often been under attack in Washington, DC. The question of whether climate change is a threat got caught in battles between environmental activists and politicians for a long time. It wasn't until the very hot summer of 1988, when NASA scientist James Hansen told senators at a hearing that human-caused global warming was imminent, that Congress started to take the issue more seriously.

Scientists recover a deep-sea mooring system that had been recording changes in temperature and other characteristics of Arctic Ocean waters.

What about other countries?

Other countries have long been concerned about the issue of climate change. These countries became convinced that a solution should be explored that involved as many other nations as possible. In 1972, at the first World Summit in Sweden, countries decided to meet every 10 years to assess the health of the earth.

Twenty years later, at the Earth Summit in Brazil, dozens of countries were given the task of coming up with an agreement that would slow down the flow of human-caused greenhouse gases into the atmosphere. They met in Kyoto, Japan, at a conference sponsored by the United Nations in 1997.

The deal that emerged in Kyoto was that within 15 years, the 38 major industrialized nations, including the United States, would have to reduce their overall emissions of greenhouse gases below the levels they were in 1990.

To meet the targets, a credit-trading system was set up in which countries could buy credits by helping other countries. For example, if a developing country uses renewable energy or renovates its fossil-fuel burning plants to reduce emissions, that country can sell its credits to industrialized countries and use the money to boost its own economy.

Why was the Kyoto agreement controversial?

It didn't treat all countries equally. While the United States had to reduce its emissions, large developing countries like China and India didn't—even though their economies are growing very fast. This caused (and still causes) resentment among U.S. politicians.

Some critics of the agreement didn't like the credit-buying system. They said it allowed the rich countries—the ones most responsible for the biggest greenhouse gas emissions in the first place—to basically buy their way out of meeting their commitments.

The Kyoto agreement expires in 2012. The United States and many other countries met in Copenhagen, Denmark, in 2009 to discuss a new one, but they didn't make as much progress as they had hoped.

What's been happening in the United States since the Kyoto agreement?

The Environmental Protection Agency (EPA) said in 2003 that greenhouse gases from global warming didn't constitute an air pollutant within the meaning of the U.S. Clean Air Act, the law that ensures the cleanliness of the air we breathe. This was the opposite of its opinion when Bill Clinton was president—and led to a court challenge from cities, states, and environmental groups.

But the Supreme Court decided in an important ruling in 2007 that the gases that cause global warming *are* pollutants under the Clean Air Act. The court also found that the U.S. government has the authority to regulate carbon dioxide and other heat-trapping gases. In 2009, the EPA officially adopted the position that carbon dioxide and other greenhouse gas emissions pose a danger to the public's health.

What does President Obama want to do about global warming?

President Obama wants greenhouse emissions in 2020 to be the same as they were in 1990 and 80 percent below these levels by 2050. He supports a program that allows businesses to trade among themselves for the right to emit greenhouse gases as long as they remain within certain limits. This is called a *cap and trade* system.

A cap and trade system works sort of like a weekly allowance from your parents. Companies are either given or buy credits entitling them to give off a specific amount of carbon. A baseline target, or cap, is established that they can't exceed. Here's the difference from an allowance, though: companies that fall below the cap can either sell their credits to other companies or save them to use later.

Another way to lower greenhouse gas emissions that some politicians prefer is a *carbon tax*, a tax placed on the use of coal, oil, and other fossil fuels that is usually based on their carbon content. This way is designed to reduce usage rather than just raise money like other kinds of taxes. But the idea is controversial because taxes generally aren't popular and Congress is wary of approving them.

President Obama also is spending money to develop and put in place *renewable energy* programs (wind, solar power and others)

Talking to Politicians About Climate Change

For some teenagers, watching the news to hear politicians talk about climate change hasn't been enough. They've gone directly to the politicians.

One of them is Verner Wilson, a Yup'ik Eskimo from Dillingham, Alaska. Even though Alaska is very cold, he has learned that gradual warming has caused many problems there: in 2005, the state saw a record low amount of sea ice, which is a protective barrier to coastal communities in Alaska against harsh winter storms.

While he was in high school, Verner joined Alaska Youth for Environmental Action, a program of the National Wildlife Federation. They organized a petition drive and in 2006 collected more than 5,000 signatures from other teenagers in more than 130 cities and towns across the state, asking for action.

that can bring down the amount of greenhouse gases released into the atmosphere. He wants the United States to become less dependent on oil and to work closely with other countries on ways to fight climate change, including making sure that poor countries have access to programs that do so.

What have states been doing?

A lot. States have been putting in their own programs to reduce carbon dioxide and other greenhouse gas emissions. These programs range from laws that require an increasing proportion of the state's energy to come from renewable—and much lower-emitting—fuel sources like solar and wind energy to other incentives to encourage the use of lower emissions. The programs are also funding new technologies for cars.

More than 30 states offer electric customers the option of "green pricing," which means customers pay more on their electric bills to have some or all of their energy provided by renewable sources. Even more states allow customers who have their own electricity systems, like rooftop solar panels, to sell the electricity they don't use back to their local electric utility.

States are even banding together with their neighbors for solutions. In 2005, a group of northeastern states (Maine, New Hampshire, Vermont, Connecticut, Delaware, New York, and New Jersey) started a system to control global-warming pollution. Other states, like New Mexico, Arizona, Washington, and Oregon, have signed similar agreements to work with each other.

What about cities?

Cities are getting into the act too. More than 900 mayors have agreed to take part in a program launched by the mayor of Seattle in 2005 to take local steps to reduce global-warming pollution. Among the cities is Evanston, Illinois, north of Chicago, which passed a resolution requiring that 20 percent of its energy come from renewable sources. Meanwhile, Warwick, Rhode Island, replaced all 113 traffic lights and 59 crosswalk signals with lower-cost lights designed to reduce carbon emissions. The city estimates the move will save tens of thousands of dollars every year.

And some of the largest cities, like New York, Chicago, Los Angeles, and Philadelphia, joined in 2006 with former President Clinton and leaders of other cities around the world, like London and Cairo, to buy cheaper energy-efficient products and share ideas. To find out what your city is doing, go to www.coolcities.us.

Local governments are also trying to get people to take public transportation—buses and trains—to reduce car usage. These governments are adopting "smart growth" planning strategies to create livable areas in and around the centers of cities, where people have lots of options other than just driving to get around easily.

They then traveled to Washington, DC, to deliver those signatures to members of Congress. Not all of the politicians agreed with the group. But Verner and the others say they were able to persuade some politicians that something must be done.

"This is our generation's issue," says Verner, who later became a student at Brown University. "We're going to be the ones who are paying for it."

In "smart growth" areas like this one in Washington, DC, people can walk to businesses near where they live.

Verner Wilson wants more young people to address climate change.

Why do politicians care more about climate change lately?

One reason is the scientific findings that have come out about the potential dire effects of increased warming. Another is research showing that global warming may be contributing to more intense storms and could lead to a repeat of tragedies like Hurricane Katrina, which destroyed much of New Orleans and other Gulf Coast areas in 2005. Meanwhile, lawmakers who support nuclear power see an opportunity to promote its use as a solution. Nuclear energy doesn't cause any greenhouse gas emissions.

Former vice president Al Gore.

A final reason has been the media giving much more attention to climate change. That helped lead to the success of Gore's movie *An Inconvenient Truth*, which won the Academy Award in 2007 for Best Documentary and won Gore the Nobel Peace Prize with the Intergovernmental Panel on Climate Change.

What else has Gore been saying?

He wants to reduce carbon dioxide by 90 percent from current levels by 2050. He also wants to stop building any new coal-fired power plants that can't use technologies to reduce emissions. And he suggests creating an "Electranet," a new way of getting electricity into homes and businesses that allows individuals and business to feed power back into the system.

"A day will come when our children and grandchildren will look back and they'll ask one of two questions," Gore told members of Congress in 2007. "Either they will ask, 'What in God's name were they doing? Didn't they see the evidence? Didn't they realize that four times in 15 years, the entire scientific community of this world issued unanimous reports calling upon them to act? What was wrong with them?'

"Or they'll ask another question. They may look back and they'll say, 'How did they find the uncommon moral courage to rise above politics and redeem the promise of American democracy and do what some said was impossible and shake things up and tell the special interests, Okay, we've heard you and we're going to do the best we can to take your considerations into account, but we're going to do what's right?'"

Become a Movie Critic for Global Warming

Get a copy of *An Inconvenient Truth* and watch it. Invite some friends if you'd like. Afterward, ask the following questions:

What was most surprising to you about the movie? Why?

Did you understand everything that Gore was talking about? What left you confused?

How did it change your feelings? Are you more certain that global warming is a big problem, or would you like to hear from more people?

Did seeing the movie cause you to want to do anything about global warming?

ACTIVITY

CHAPTER 6

What Are People Doing About Climate Change?

Is anyone doing anything about climate change?

Yes, a lot of things are happening outside of government. Some of them are for reasons other than reducing greenhouse gas emissions, like controlling high gasoline prices. Changes include:

Making wider use of renewable energy sources, like solar and wind, that don't burn oil, coal, and other fossil fuels.

Making appliances like refrigerators and air conditioners—and also homes and other buildings—more energy efficient.

Designing cars and trucks that give off less—or no—carbon dioxide.

Developing ways to store carbon inside the earth or oceans instead of letting it escape into the atmosphere.

But it's important to remember that *there's no one, easy solution* to climate change. Solving the climate change problem will take a combination of approaches, over a long time, to tackle it.

Will solving climate change take lots of new technology?

Not necessarily, but it will take much more widespread use of what we do now. "I believe with technology pretty much available today, or in the very near short term . . . we could get a 30 to 40 percent reduction in greenhouse gases," Dana Christensen, an official at Tennessee's Oak Ridge National Laboratory, told the *Washington Post*. Oak Ridge is one of the places where the U.S. government conducts scientific research.

The challenge is putting these technologies all over the planet so they can be effective, said Rutgers University professor Anthony Broccoli, a contributor to the Intergovernmental Panel on Climate Change. "It's going to be very difficult to rapidly reduce the emission of carbon dioxide, because we don't have the technologies available at the proper scale to do this immediately," Broccoli told the New Jersey newspaper the *Star-Ledger*.

How does renewable energy contribute to slowing climate change?

Renewable energy effectively uses sunlight, wind, rain, tides, and geothermal (underground) heat, which are naturally replenished and don't directly emit greenhouse gases. Renewable energy technologies include solar power, wind power, hydroelectricity, and biomass (plant materials and animal waste that can be used as fuel) and biofuels (fuel made from renewable resources such as cellulose, corn or plant oils) for transportation. Right now, renewables account for only a small percentage of the energy used in the United States. Most

Wind turbines are seen as a key way to combat global warming.

of our energy comes from fossil fuels like coal and oil. We are so dependent on fossil fuels that even if the solar energy industry grew 30 percent a year, it would still account for only around 9 percent of our total energy use by 2025.

Alternative sources aren't always perfect. For example, biofuels like ethanol (which is usually made from corn) were originally thought to be better than fossil fuels because the carbon released when they burned was balanced by the carbon absorbed when the plants were used to make the fuels grow. But scientists have learned that many biofuels can cause *more* greenhouse gas emissions than fossil fuels because of the need to clear lands to grow them, which leads to the release of more carbon dioxide.

Which renewable sources are likely to be used more?

Wind power is one of the sources whose technology is no longer experimental. It could provide as much as 20 percent of the United States' energy needs. Wind power already provides almost that much in Denmark, and it's being used more frequently in Germany, Spain, and China.

Most modern wind turbines have three blades and operate facing into the wind. The wind turns the blades, which spin a shaft that connects to a generator and makes electricity. A five-megawatt turbine can produce enough energy to power more than 1,400 households.

Are there problems with it?

Some people don't like the sight of giant wind turbines, whose blades can be longer than 80 feet (24 meters). Turbines can kill birds and bats flying into them, though newer models are being built to be safer. Also, people argue wind energy can't replace other energy sources because—obviously—the wind doesn't always blow. So they say it needs to be backed up by more reliable fossil fuel plants.

But wind energy advocates say in response that if you put enough wind turbines up, the wind will always be blowing somewhere and so you won't have to rely on just a few.

Solar panels are becoming increasingly common atop homes and office buildings.

What about solar energy?

That also shows promise. Sunlight is not only the most plentiful energy resource on the earth, it's also one of the most versatile, converting readily to electricity.

Light from the sun consists of particles called *photons*. As photons are absorbed by solar panels on top of homes and offices, electricity is produced. When the panels generate more electricity than is needed, the excess power gets sent to the electricity grid, which provides power on cloudy days or at night.

The challenge is to bring down the cost of solar power and increase how much power is converted from absorbed light to electrical energy. Some scientists are even studying solar power generation from space, where the sun is many times more intense than on the earth. Space solar power already provides energy to satellites and space stations that orbit the earth.

What about hydroelectric power?

Hydroelectric power is created by the force of water driving an electricity generator. It usually comes from dams, which create reservoirs. But hydroelectric power can cause problems for wildlife: studies have shown that dams have reduced salmon populations by preventing access to the salmons' spawning grounds upstream. Also, dams increase the amount of plant matter that decomposes and produces methane, a greenhouse gas. So some environmentalists are wary of hydroelectric power.

Nevada's Hoover Dam is perhaps the country's best-known dam.

What about other alternative sources?

Going into detail about all alternative power sources would require another book or two. But we do need to make special mention of nuclear power because it's been cited so much as a big solution to climate change. Its advocates call it the one existing source of energy that can generate massive amounts of electricity without causing any air pollution or greenhouse gas emissions.

Nuclear power accounts for about 19 percent of the electricity generated in the United States. That's about as much as all the electricity used in California, Texas, and New York. Some countries are even more heavily dependent on nuclear energy; France gets about three-quarters of its power from it.

A nuclear power plant operates in much the same way as a fossil fuel plant, with one important difference: the source of heat. The process that produces the heat in a nuclear plant is the fissioning, or splitting, of uranium atoms. The heat boils water to make the steam that turns the generator, just as in a fossil fuel plant. The part of the plant where the heat is produced is called the reactor core.

Nuclear power is a controversial potential global-warming solution.

What don't people like about nuclear power?

Nuclear power generates leftover wastes that are highly radioactive, so they're very difficult to store easily. The U.S. government has studied burying waste from power plants inside a hollowed-out mountain in the Nevada desert called Yucca Mountain, but a lot of people in that state (and other states along the routes where the waste would be shipped from) don't like the idea and want other options studied instead.

Critics also worry about nuclear material getting in the hands of terrorists or other countries that could make bombs with it and that accidents could release radioactive material. No new nuclear plants were built in the United States for many years after a serious accident in 1979 at Pennsylvania's Three Mile Island plant. Nuclear power plants also cost a lot of money to build compared to other kinds of energy sources.

Nevertheless, some environmentalists argue that nuclear power has so much potential that these risks are worth taking. The U.S. government has gone to great lengths in recent years to try to make nuclear power a viable option. Expect to hear a lot more about it.

How are appliances helping to reduce global warming?

Household appliances, including the thirstiest energy users among them, have been steadily reducing how much energy they use. Today's new kitchen refrigerators use 70 percent less power than the ones made in the 1970s.

Many companies are making furnaces, air conditioners, washing machines, dishwashers, refrigerators, and other big appliances that qualify for the U.S. government's Energy Star label, which shows they save energy. In some cases, those appliances exceed the standard by 50 percent.

The problem is that consumers often pay no attention to energy use when they're shopping. For example, computers can be made to use less power, but since most people don't put that on the list of qualities important to them, manufacturers don't see a pressing need to spend extra money on making their computers more energy efficient.

Are cars being made to reduce global warming?

Yes, and more are coming. Here are three basic types of cars of the future:

Hybrid-electric vehicle: It uses a regular engine for most of its power but also has an electric motor run by batteries recharged by the engine.

You probably know about the Toyota Prius, the first mass-produced hybrid car. During its lifetime, it emits an estimated 110,000 pounds (5,000 kilograms) of carbon dioxide, including the amount put out during manufacturing. That compares with 180,000 pounds (81,000 kilograms) for a Toyota Camry and 310,000 pounds (139,500 kilograms) for a Toyota Tundra pickup truck.

Toyota's Prius has become a popular way for car buyers to reduce global warming.

Sales of the Prius have gone up dramatically in the United States, from around 15,500 in 2001 to more than 150,000 in 2008. Other car companies have noticed the trend and introduced more hybrid brands.

But many people still prefer to buy sport-utility vehicles (SUVs), which burn 45 percent more fuel than regular cars. Until the demand changes, U.S. automakers say, it's very hard to commit to making a lot more hybrid cars than they are now. (They are starting to make more hybrid SUVs.)

Making more hybrid cars has caused a hugely controversial debate because the auto industry has been struggling economically and its supporters worry a lot about being forced to abandon cars that are making money. But everyone agrees there must eventually be change: cars and trucks produce 30 percent of the world's carbon dioxide emissions. Right now, about 800 million cars are in active use all over the world. By 2050, as cars become more common in China and India, it'll be 3.25 billion.

Plug-in hybrid-electric vehicle:
This vehicle is a hybrid that can charge its batteries by being plugged into a charger, allowing all-electric trips. Chevrolet has developed an electric car of this type called the Volt. A British company already has developed the Tesla Roadster, a sports car that can travel 221 miles (356 kilometers) on a single battery charge.

Chevrolet's Volt is seen as a way to reduce greenhouse gas emissions.

Battery-electric vehicle: This is an electric car powered entirely by batteries without a backup engine as in regular cars. Some of these were produced in the 1990s, but automakers have decided to focus more on hybrids.

What else is being planned with cars?

Some research has been done on hydrogen-powered fuel cells that could be used to power cars. A fuel cell is an *electrochemical device*, like a battery. It converts the chemicals hydrogen and oxygen into water, and in the process it produces electricity.

A battery eventually loses its power, and you either have to toss it out or recharge it. But as long as there's a flow of chemicals into a fuel cell, electricity flows out of the cell. And all that comes out of the car's tailpipe is water vapor.

The U.S. government has been working with universities and private companies on fuel cell technology—not just to power cars but homes, cell phones, and other devices. Ford has developed a fuel cell car that can drive 350 miles (564 kilometers) on a single fill-up, and Chevrolet has tested its own version.

Stealing Carbon Dioxide from the Air

Can carbon dioxide be taken from the air and converted into gasoline? That's what some scientists are trying to find out.

Two scientists at New Mexico's Los Alamos National Laboratory, Jeffrey Martin and William Kubic, have proposed a concept called Green Freedom. It involves blowing air over a liquid solution of potassium carbonate, which would absorb the carbon dioxide.

The carbon dioxide would then be extracted and subjected to chemical reactions that turn it into fuel. "Our concept enhances U.S. energy security . . . by reducing

But it's still going to be a while before fuel cell cars start showing up regularly on car lots. Hydrogen has to be produced—it isn't something like coal or oil that comes from the earth—and can be very expensive.

Are people talking about ways to stop carbon from reaching the atmosphere?

Yes. It's called *sequestration* and can be done in different ways.

Carbon is sequestered, or stored, by forests naturally. Forests act as big storehouses of carbon dioxide when they're increasing in size or becoming dense with trees. Trees and other plants soak up the carbon that would otherwise rise and trap heat in the atmosphere. Reforestation—planting large numbers of trees—can help slow the effects of climate change. Reforestation also has other benefits, like helping wildlife and conserving soil.

Scientists are looking at ways that sequestration could be done artificially through "carbon capture and storage" programs. Engineers are trying to capture the carbon spewing from coal-fired power plants and industrial smokestacks and bury it deep within the earth or the oceans. Some studies suggest that this could play a huge

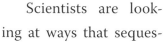

Above: Carbon sequestration by direct injection into the ocean involves the capture, separation, transport, and injection of carbon dioxide from land or tankers.

role in fighting global warming, and some countries are looking into it.

Critics point out possible problems with carbon capture. They cite the risks to people from the release of stored gas from underground at toxic levels, the potential for drinking water contamination, and other problems. They would rather focus on holding down the production of carbon dioxide. Some say it should only be a temporary "stopgap" while other long-term technologies are developed.

What about changes in buildings?

Companies are designing smarter, more energy-efficient buildings. They note that building a new 50,000-square-foot (4,500-square-meter) office building (that's about the same size as a supermarket) releases as much carbon into the atmosphere as driving a car 2.8 million miles (4.5 million kilometers).

Buildings can be made with efficient materials like old-fashioned straw covered with stucco or new *polystyrene* boards instead of plywood. Buildings can also be constructed using insulation that boosts energy savings as well as with fewer leaks, windows that reject heat and admit light, and designs that make the most of the sun's energy. Those designs can be as simple as making sure every desk in an office gets some sunlight.

Some people are going even further. They're designing "living houses" in which the walls and roof are formed from living trees and renewable energy sources like solar are used inside. Even something as simple as white roofs on houses has been shown to make a difference. As one researcher at the U.S. government's Lawrence Berkeley

dependence on imported oil," Martin said.

The concept still needs to be tested, but some experts think it has a lot of potential in the years to come. Other scientists have proposed similar ideas.

Klaus Lackner, a Columbia University professor and inventor, has come up with a prototype of a "mechanical tree" that can sop up carbon dioxide. It doesn't look like a tree, but it does some of the same things that trees do in extracting the greenhouse gas. Once carbon dioxide is collected, it can be injected underground to help force out oil.

Lackner hopes that within a few years, he can produce a mechanical tree that can be sold widely and is easily transported. The current version is about nine feet (2.7 meters) tall, but others would need to be much larger to make a significant dent in reducing carbon dioxide.

"Our goal is to get the mechanical tree down to the size of a trailer truck so you can move it wherever you want," he said.

Opposite page: A prototype of an air extractor that removes carbon dioxide, with Allen Wright, president of the company building the device.

National Laboratory estimated, if we took all the roofs and pavement in the world's large cities and either painted them white or replaced the black asphalt with brighter material, increasing their solar reflectivity, the global cooling effect would be about the same as taking all the world's cars off the road for 11 years.

What future inventions are being explored?

Even though scientists say we can attack climate change mostly with existing technology, some are still trying to develop new techniques to combat it. A variety of "geo-engineering" proposals are drawing increased attention as a kind of backstop in case efforts to reduce the amount of greenhouse gases generated don't work out as hoped. Among the ideas:

Dumping tons of iron into the ocean to try to stimulate the growth of phytoplankton, microscopic plants that absorb carbon dioxide. But critics say the decaying plants release nitrous oxide—another greenhouse gas.

Sending electric currents through seawater to separate the salt into sodium and chloride. The chloride molecules bond with the hydrogen in the water and create hydrochloric acid, which is then removed. That leaves more sodium in the water, which means the ocean can absorb more carbon dioxide. That process also has its problems: it could create molecules that destroy the ozone layer.

Some astronomers propose to cool the earth by sending up 16 trillion tiny mirrors to reflect sunlight back into space. It would cost trillions of dollars.

If all this leaves you wondering what *you* can do, we'll discuss that in the next chapter.

CHAPTER 7

What Can I Do About Climate Change?

Is there anything I can do to fight climate change?

Yes. Just remember that there's no one, magical solution. Fighting climate change will take a variety of solutions, from many people over many years, to lower greenhouse gas emissions. This causes some people to get discouraged—but it shouldn't deter you.

These bulbs are one way to reduce global warming.

You and your family might already be doing some of the following energy-saving measures to help the environment. But knowing that they help reduce your carbon footprint is another reason to keep on doing them.

Change lightbulbs: This is one of the easiest, most common ways to reduce energy use. Low-energy fluorescent lightbulbs (they sometimes look kind of squiggly) use less than 20 percent of the energy of a conventional incandescent lightbulb and can last up to 15 times longer. Replacing three frequently used incandescent bulbs with fluorescent bulbs can cut 300 pounds (135 kilograms) of carbon dioxide a year.

If everyone on the planet switched to these kinds of bulbs, it would stop 16 billion tons (17.6 metric tons) of carbon from entering the atmosphere over the next 25 years. That's more than all of the carbon now being released by humans into the atmosphere in *two years*.

Turn off appliances: Speaking of lightbulbs, you can also remember to turn them off when you don't need them—along with computers, TVs, and other appliances. That can save you around 500 pounds (225 kilograms) of carbon a year. Turning off just one 60-watt bulb that would otherwise burn eight hours a day can save 1,000 pounds (450 kilograms) of carbon over the lifetime of the bulb.

Drying clothes can reduce electricity, which in turn helps the climate.

Use a clothesline: You can save electricity in other ways. One is very simple—hanging up laundry to dry instead of putting it in a clothes dryer. (That's how people did it in the old days.) That's good for 700 pounds (315 kilograms) of carbon a year. If all Americans line-dried for just half a year, it would save more than 3 percent of the country's total output of carbon dioxide from homes.

Fill up the dryer: If you have to use a dryer—or a washing machine or dishwasher—make sure that it's full. Don't just use it for partial loads. A full dishwasher can save you 100 pounds (45 kilograms) of carbon a year.

Buy energy-efficient products: Look for the government's Energy Star logo on what your family buys. Its website, energystar.gov, has a list. The label is now on more than 50 kinds of products, including major appliances, office equipment, lighting, and home electronics. The government has extended the label to cover new homes and commercial and industrial buildings.

Energy Star logo.

Reduce standby power: Did you know that about one-quarter of the energy a television uses is when it isn't turned on? You can save energy by unplugging TVs, DVD players, cell phone chargers, and other appliances and electronics when you don't need them. Even putting your computer in sleep mode instead of using a screen saver is good for almost 1,100 pounds (495 kilograms) a year. And don't forget that power strips save energy.

Cut back on hot water: No, you don't have to take cold showers all the time, but taking showers rather than baths conserves hot water. Heating up water takes energy. And washing your clothes in cold water instead of warm or hot is good for 500 pounds (225 kilograms) of annual carbon savings.

Adjust your thermostat: Can you deal with wearing an extra sweater during the winter and opening the windows in the summer? Not only will your parents be saving on their monthly bills, but turning a thermostat down one degree F. (0.6 degree C.) cooler than normal can reduce carbon emissions from electric generation plants by more than 1,150 pounds (518 kilograms) a year.

Cut down on car rides: You can save energy by walking, biking, or taking the bus instead of riding in a car. Walking and biking are good for your health, too.

When you do ride in a car, ask your parents and other family members to keep it tuned up regularly and to watch how fast they go. Gas mileage goes down as you get over 60 miles per hour (97 kilometers per hour). Using cruise control can save 600 pounds (270 kilograms) of carbon a year. And if someone you know is looking to

Riding a bike or walking instead of driving both reduce greenhouse gas emissions.

buy a new car, try to get them to consider a hybrid instead of an SUV or larger vehicle.

You also can ask car drivers to take part in a carbon offsetting program. At Terrapass.com, you can calculate your vehicle's carbon dioxide emissions, then buy a TerraPass, which will offset your contributions by contributing to wind, solar energy, and other greenhouse gas reduction efforts.

Eat locally grown food: Estimates on how long food travels from the pasture to your plate range between 1,200 and 2,500 miles (1,932 and 4,025 kilometers). Eating locally grown food means less fossil fuel burned in shipping and preparing it. So that might mean giving up grapes for the winter, but it could save you as much 5,000 pounds (2,250 kilograms) of carbon a year.

Bag groceries in reusable bags: Americans use more than 12 million barrels of oil each year to produce plastic grocery bags. Many of the bags get thrown away after one use, going to landfills, where

they take many years to decompose. Paper bags require cutting down trees, which releases carbon dioxide. Use reusable cloth tote bags for shopping.

Plant a tree: Planting a tree is a fun, easy way to reduce greenhouse gases. Trees absorb carbon dioxide from the air. Numerous organizations offer regular chances to plant trees.

Planting trees is good for the environment for many reasons.

Recycle: Recycle cans, bottles, plastic bags, and newspapers. When you recycle, you send less trash to the landfill. Producing new paper, glass, and metal products like cans from recyclable materials can save up to 90 percent of the energy, pollution, and greenhouse emissions that would happen from using

Spreading the Message of Change

After 13-year-old Alec Loorz of Ventura, California, saw the movie *An Inconvenient Truth*, he knew he had to do something about climate change.

But it didn't just involve switching lightbulbs—he wanted to tell other kids how important it is to fight the growth in carbon dioxide emissions. "I felt really pumped up about it," he recalls.

Alec asked Al Gore's office if he could be among those trained to give the same presentation that the former vice president gives in the movie. But he was told he was too young. So he started an organization called Kids Vs. Global Warming and created a website, kids-vs-

Alec Loorz gives a speech on climate change.

brand-new materials. If you recycled half of your household waste, that's good for 2,400 pounds (1,080 kilograms) of annual carbon savings.

Here's an interesting statistic: China is already the world's most populous country, and it's growing fast. If the Chinese eventually use as much paper as we now do in the United States, they'll need twice as much as the entire world now produces. And that's just *one* country.

Compost: Compost piles cut down on the amount of garbage that gets hauled away and tossed in landfills. Just remember to keep it free of meat, fish, and other animal products if you don't want to attract insects.

Read: Many books and even more websites are devoted to the issue of climate change. Here are just a few of the most popular and relatively easy-to-understand books:

A–Z of Global Warming, by Simon Rosser
  (Schmall World Publishing, 2008)
The Hot Topic, by Gabrielle Walker and David King
  (Harvest Books, 2008)
Six Degrees, by Mark Lynas (National Geographic, 2008)
An Inconvenient Truth, by Al Gore (Viking Rodale, 2007)
Field Notes from a Catastrophe, by Elizabeth Kolbert
  (Bloomsbury, 2006)
The Weather Makers, by Tim Flannery (Grove Press,
  2005)

Here are some of the many websites on climate change out there:

GOVERNMENT

Intergovernmental Panel on Climate Change:
www.ipcc.ch

Environmental Protection Agency: www.epa.gov/
climatechange/index.html

National Oceanic and Atmospheric Administration:
www.noaa.gov/climate.html

NASA: www.nasa.gov

Global Change Research Program:
www.usgcrp.gov/usgcrp/

House Select Committee for Energy Independence and
Global Warming: globalwarming.house.gov

National Academy of Sciences: www.nas.edu

ENVIRONMENTAL

Al Gore's website: www.climatecrisis.net

Environmental Defense's climate information blog:
www.environmentaldefenseblogs.org/climate411

Union of Concerned Scientists: www.ucsusa.org/
global_warming/science

Greenpeace: www.greenpeace.org

Sierra Club: www.sierraclub.org/globalwarming

Friends of the Earth: www.foe.org

National Wildlife Federation: www.nwf.org/
globalwarming

U.S. Climate Action Partnership: www.us-cap.org

It's Getting Hot in Here—Dispatches from the Youth
Climate Movement: www.itsgettinghotinhere.org

global-warming.com, to provide information in a way they could understand it.

He read all he could and met with scientists who study global warming. Soon he began giving speeches at his school and to other schools around Southern California—even some colleges. (You can see videos of his speeches on YouTube.)

"Ask most kids and they may not be able to tell you exactly what carbon dioxide is or why burning fossil fuels adds greenhouse gases to the atmosphere, but they can tell you that they are afraid of what will happen in their lifetime if we don't stop doing it," Alec said in one of his presentations.

He firmly believes that kids shouldn't wait to take action. "People tell me all the time, 'It's great to have kids involved. You kids are the future.' And it's true—we are the future," he said. "But we are more than that. We are the present. We are important members of society right now. And our voices do make a difference."

Other kids are making their voices heard too.

Another 13-year-old, Scott Syroka of Johnston, Iowa, also was motivated by *An Inconvenient Truth* to do something about climate change. He has worked with the Sierra Club and other organizations to tell politicians how strongly he feels, and worked on some of their political campaigns.

Scott also has marched in public rallies to call more attention to the issue and intends to work on it throughout his lifetime.

"I am extremely optimistic with how people my age can respond to this problem," Scott says.

Former U.S. senator John Edwards (left) and Scott Syroka (right).

OTHER WEBSITES

Pew Center on Climate Change: www.pewclimate.org

Real Climate: www.realclimate.org

Climate Institute: www.climate.org

Science Daily climate news: www.sciencedaily.com/news/earth_climate/global_warming

New York Times' "Dot Earth" blog: dotearth.blogs.nytimes.com

American Council for an Energy Efficient Economy: www.aceee.org

Kids Global Climate Change Institute: kidsgcci.ning.com

Top 100 Climate Change Sites: www.world.org/weo/climate

Talk: Many middle and junior high schools, high schools, and colleges have started global-warming clubs—groups where interested students can learn more about the science and discuss ways to address the problem. Those clubs have asked the officials at their schools to take serious steps to reduce their carbon footprint.

Hundreds of schools have agreed to do so. The National Wildlife Federation sponsors the Campus Climate Challenge, which recognizes schools that have made progress each year. Most entrants are colleges, but some high schools have won awards too.

One is the Berkshire School, a boarding school in western Massachusetts. It has been hailed for its aggressive climate action plan, which includes everything from retrofitting dorms with energy-efficient windows, to recycling a wide variety of materials, to leasing low-emissions school vehicles. All of that has sharply cut the school's carbon dioxide emissions in recent years.

Consider climate change from a global perspective: The United States pumps far more carbon dioxide into the atmosphere than other countries, yet many of those countries will be hit much harder than the United States by global warming. Is that fair?

To many activists, the disproportionate role that the United States has played in causing the problem has to be included in the thinking about what is to be done to solve it.

Learning More About Global Warming and Climate Change in School

If you'd like to learn more about this subject in your school, the Environmental Protection Agency (EPA) has a classroom activity kit for middle school teachers who plan to make climate change part of what they teach. The kit includes a handheld wheel to give students a way to calculate their household greenhouse gas emissions as well as discussion topics and assignments. More information can be found at **www.epa.gov/climatechange/downloads/ActivityKit.pdf.**

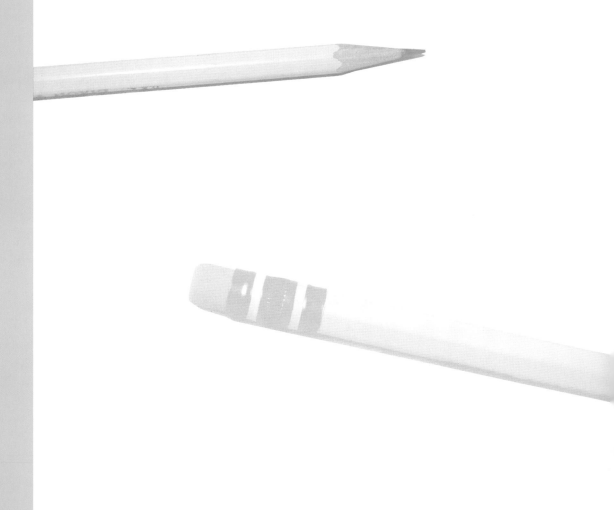

ACTIVITY

Glossary

Albedo: The amount of light that a body or surface reflects and the amount of light that is absorbed.

Atmosphere: The layer of air surrounding the earth.

Barren: Land without any trees or other plants.

Cap and trade: A system in which companies have to meet a target of greenhouse gas emissions; if the target is met, they can trade credits so one company can emit more and another less.

Carbon dioxide: A colorless, odorless gas that is the main substance responsible for human-caused global warming.

Carbon footprint: The amount of carbon dioxide each person produces or uses.

Carbon tax: A tax placed on the use of coal, oil, and other fossil fuels that is usually based on their carbon content.

Climate: The average and common weather conditions over a period beyond a few weeks.

Climate change: Global warming as well as other changes in climate that might occur as a result of warming, like sea level rise and extreme weather.

Electrochemical device: A device that converts chemical energy into electrical energy (or electrical energy into chemical energy) through a chemical reaction.

Emissions: The release or discharge of a substance (like carbon dioxide) into the environment.

Endangered: Animal species that are dwindling in numbers and may go extinct soon.

Fossil fuels: Fuels formed many thousands of years ago from decayed plants and animals. Oil, coal, and natural gas are such fuels.

Feedback: A process resulting from climate change that may increase (positive feedback) or diminish (negative feedback) the magnitude of climate change.

Feedback loop: A circular pathway of cause and effect that can result from climate change. For example, global warming can shorten the season for exploration of coal, oil, and natural gas. This can lead to smaller gas reserves and more coal burning, leading to greater warming.

Food web: In an ecosystem, energy and materials flow around in a web from plants to animals. Plants get energy from the sun and materials from the soil to grow, and then animals get energy and materials to grow by eating plants and each other. Finally decomposers, like fungi, break down dead plants and animals and recycle the materials into soil, ready to be made into new plants and animals.

Global warming: The changes in temperature in the earth's air and oceans that are making the world hotter. Because it's happening so fast as a result of humans' actions, some prefer to call it *global heating, global climate disruption,* or *global weirding.*

Greenhouse effect: What carbon dioxide and other gases do to the climate. These gases act like a blanket covering the earth and keep us warm.

Ice ages: Periods when the earth was covered by huge amounts of ice from glaciers, the moving masses of ice and snow that pile up without melting.

Lobbyist: A person outside of government who tries to influence how laws and policies are made.

Nutrient: A material that serves as food or provides nourishment for people, animals, and plants.

Old growth: A forest that has not been logged in which the trees are at least 150 years old.

Ozone hole: Not a circular hole, but an area of the atmosphere, over the North and South poles, from which ozone has been depleted.

Parts per million: The number of "parts" by weight of a substance per million parts of water. This unit is commonly used to represent the amount of harmful substances in the environment.

Photon: A particle of light.

Polystyrene: A type of plastic foam used in insulation, plates, cups, and disposable (throwaway) food containers.

Proxies: Methods of determining values like temperatures and rainfall by using substitutes.

Renewable energy: Energy resources like wind power or solar energy that can keep producing indefinitely without running out.

Sequestration: A method of removing carbon dioxide from the atmosphere, either through biological processes like those of trees and other plants or geological processes through storage of carbon dioxide in underground reservoirs.

Sinks: Areas like forests, grasslands, and oceans that naturally take up carbon dioxide from the atmosphere.

Snowpack: The total snow and ice on the ground, including both the new snow and the previous snow and ice that haven't melted.

Vapor: The gas given off by a solid or liquid substance at ordinary temperatures.

Waterways: Bodies of water like rivers, lakes, and oceans that ships can use.

Wavelength: The distance from the crest of one wave to the crest of the next. Radiation from the sun can be measured in wavelengths.

Weather: The current conditions of temperature as well as humidity, wind, and precipitation (rain or snowfall).

Illustration Credits

page 49:   National Oceanic and Atmospheric Administration.

page 50:   PhotoDisc by Getty Images.

page 53:   PhotoDisc by Getty Images.

page 54:   US Geological Survey.

page 55:   National Oceanic and Atmospheric Administration.

page 56:   US Fish and Wildlife Service.

page 59:   PhotoDisc by Getty Images.

page 62:   State of California.

page 65:   National Oceanic and Atmospheric Administration.

page 66–67: PhotoDisc by Getty Images.

page 69:   Liisa Ecola.

page 69:   Courtesy Verner Wilson.

page 70:   US House of Representatives.

page 71:   PhotoDisc by Getty Images.

page 75:   Sandia National Laboratories.

page 76:   Energy Information Administration.

page 77:   US Bureau of Reclamation.

page 78:   US Nuclear Regulatory Commission.

page 80:   Wikimedia Commons.

page 81:   Wikimedia Commons.

page 82:   Lawrence Berkeley Laboratory.

page 82:   Courtesy Global Research Technologies.

page 85:   Wikimedia Commons.

page 86:   Anderson Ross/Blend Images/Corbis.

page 87:   Courtesy Department of Energy.

page 88:   PhotoDisc by Getty Images.

page 89:   Luedke and Sparrow/Getty Images.

page 90:   Courtesy Alec Loorz.

page 92:   Courtesy Scott Syroka.

Index

about, 90; difference from global warming, 3–4; measuring of, 16; modeling, 16–19; potential effects of, 41–59; scientific responses to, 73–75, 77, 81–84; skepticism of, 6–8, 20, 46–47, 61; websites about, 90–92

Clinton, Bill, 67, 69

clouds, 13, 17, 19, 38

coal, 4, 10, 20, 23, 26, 30, 37, 67, 70, 73, 75, 82, 95, 96

Copenhagen 2009 climate talks, 66

coral/coral reefs, 16, 55

Crist, Charlie, 62

Energy Star, 79, 86

farms and farming, 23, 31, 33–34, 42, 50, 52, 53, 58, 60

feedbacks and feedback loops, 14, 96

Florida, 12, 33, 62; climate change effects on, 48–49

forests, 4, 31–32, 57, 58, 60, 82, 97, 98; forest fires, 48, 49; rain forests, 32–33

Fourier, Jean-Baptiste, 26

glaciers, 1, 53–54, 56, 97

global warming, 2, 5, 6, 7, 9, 13, 14, 15, 19, 20, 21, 22, 23, 25–27, 30, 32, 33, 37, 38, 41, 42, 43, 45, 47, 51, 55, 60, 65, 66, 67, 68, 69, 70, 72, 75, 79, 83, 85, 90; difference from climate change, 3–4; politicians and, 61–64; public opinions on, 8–9

golden toad, 56–57

Gore, Al, 2, 8, 61, 62, 70–71, 72, 90, 91

greenhouse effect, 3, 13, 21–26, 97; experiment, 28

greenhouse gases, 3, 4, 6, 10, 16, 18, 27, 28, 29, 30, 31, 33, 34, 35, 38, 39, 42, 46, 64, 65, 70, 73, 74, 75, 77, 78, 81, 83, 84, 85, 88, 89, 91, 94, 95; attempts to regulate, 66–68; calculation of personal emissions, 40; explanation of, 22–25

Greenland, 45, 58

Hansen, James, 65

hurricanes, 1, 43, 49, 51–52, 70

ice, 1, 6, 12, 13–14, 15, 16, 38, 42, 45, 46, 47, 48, 50, 53, 56, 57, 58, 98

ice ages, 6, 14, 20, 32, 33, 97

An Inconvenient Truth, 8, 61, 70, 72, 90, 91

India, 54, 66, 80

Industrial Revolution, 34

Inhofe, James, 61

Intergovernmental Panel on Climate Change, 2, 5, 10, 38, 42, 70, 74, 91

International Solid Waste Foundation, 39

Keeling, Charles David, 36–37

Kubic, William, 82

Kyoto Protocol, 66

Lackner, Klaus, 83

lightbulbs, 2, 85–86, 90

Live Earth, 9

Loorz, Alec, 90–91

Louisiana, climate change effects on, 49

Malawi, 43–44

Mars, 27

Martin, Jeffrey, 82

Massachusetts, climate change effects on, 50

methane, 23, 33, 39, 46

Michigan, climate change effects on, 50

National Aeronautics and Space Administration (NASA), 4, 65, 91

National Council of Churches, 45
National Oceanic and Atmospheric
    Administration, 65, 91
National Wildlife Federation, 92
natural gas, 4, 10, 30, 37, 96
Netherlands, 57
New York, climate change effects
    on, 50–51
nitrous oxide, 23
nuclear energy, 70, 77–79

Obama, Barack, 67–68
oceans, 3, 13, 14, 15, 16, 17, 30, 35,
    42, 51, 52, 58, 60, 73, 82, 84, 97,
    98; effects of warming, 54–57; sea
    level rise, 2, 3, 46, 49, 50, 55–57,
    96
oil, 4, 7, 10, 20, 30, 35, 37, 58, 67, 68,
    73, 75, 82, 83, 88, 95, 96
Oreskes, Naomi, 5
ozone, 24–26, 84, 97

Parry, Martin, 2
Pawlenty, Tim, 62
Peru, 53
polar bears, 7, 48, 57
population growth, 30, 34, 38–39

rain, 11, 12, 13, 24, 32, 33, 49, 52, 53,
    58, 74, 98
renewable/alternative energy, 66,
    67, 68, 69, 73, 74, 75, 77, 83, 98;
    hydroelectric energy, 74, 77; solar
    energy, 20, 67, 68, 74, 76–77, 83,
    84, 88, 98; wind energy, 67, 68,
    73–76, 88, 98

satellites, 18, 19, 65, 77
Schwarzenegger, Arnold, 62
Shindell, Drew, 4
Skelly, David, 58

smog, 25
sun, 3, 6, 8, 11–14, 19, 21–22, 25, 26,
    27, 28, 44, 74, 83, 84, 96, 98; heat
    waves and, 51; solar power, 20, 67,
    68, 74, 76–77, 83, 84
Syroka, Scott, 91–92

temperature, 2, 3–6, 8, 11, 13, 14, 15,
    16, 17, 18, 19, 21, 22, 25, 26, 27, 28,
    30, 32, 42, 45, 47, 58, 65, 97, 98;
    rises in states affected by climate
    change, 48–51; sea temperatures,
    54–56

United States, 5, 6, 13, 31, 34, 37, 43,
    45, 52, 53, 66, 68, 74, 75, 78, 79, 80,
    90, 93; effects of global warm-
    ing on, 47–51; responsibility for
    greenhouse gas emissions, 30,
    35, 39
U.S. Climate Action Partnership,
    64, 91
U.S. Environmental Protection
    Agency, 39, 40, 66, 67, 91
U.S. Geological Survey, 57
U.S. Global Change Research Pro-
    gram, 5

Venus, 27

Wassmann, Reiner, 34
Watt, James, 34
weather, 2, 3, 12, 17, 18, 20, 26, 32,
    36, 41, 42, 43, 46, 48, 51, 52, 58, 92,
    95, 96; difference from climate,
    11–12, 20
Wilson, Verner, 68–69
wind, 11, 13, 16, 17, 42, 46, 98

Younger Dryas, 14–15

Welcome to

Worlds of Wonder

A Young Reader's Science Series

Advisory Editors: David Holtby and Karen Taschek

In these engagingly written and beautifully illustrated books, the University of New Mexico Press seeks to convey to young readers the thrill of science as well as to inspire further inquiry into the wonders of scientific research and discovery.

ALSO AVAILABLE IN THE UNIVERSITY OF NEW MEXICO PRESS BARBARA GUTH WORLDS OF WONDER SCIENCE SERIES FOR YOUNG READERS:

Hanging with Bats: Ecobats, Vampires, and Movie Stars
by Karen Taschek
The Tree Rings' Tale: Understanding Our Changing Climate
by John Fleck